Soundings
A journal of politics and culture

Issue 49

Who will speak for England?

Editor
Jonathan Rutherford

Managing Editor
Sally Davison

Editorial Board
Stuart Hall
Ben Little
Joe Littler
Doreen Massey
Michael Rustin

Reviews Editor
George Shire

Art Editor
Tim Davison

Editorial Office
Lawrence & Wishart, 99a Wallis Road, London E9 5LN

Advertisements
Write for information to Soundings, c/o Lawrence & Wishart

Subscriptions
2012 subscription rates are (for three issues):
Institutions £125, Individuals £35

Collection as a whole © Soundings 2011
Individual articles © the authors 2011

No article may be reproduced or transmitted by any means, electronic or mechanical, including photocopying, recording or any information storage and retrieval system, without the permission in writing of the publisher, editor or author

ISSN 1362 6620
ISBN 9781907103445
Cover Photo © Mishka Henner and Liz Lock

Printed in Great Britain by Biddles, Kings Lynn
Soundings is published three times a year, in autumn, spring and summer by:
Lawrence & Wishart, 99a Wallis Road, London E9 5LN.
Email: info@lwbooks.co.uk

www.soundings.org.uk

Contents

4   Editorial

6   **Time for an optimistic Englishness**
Anthony Painter

18   **English socialism - regional accent?**
Paul Salveson

32   **Democratic localism**
Ken Spours

43   **The benefits scandal**
Kaliya Franklin and Sue Marsh

58   **'Dependency' and disability: how to misread the evidence on social security**
Declan Gaffney

73   **Cuts are a feminist issue**
The feminist fightback collective

84   **Reviews**
Craig Berry, Rhiannon Freeland, Michael Moran, Alan O'Shea

94   **Relational economics**
Andrea Westall

105   **Where did it all go wrong for George Osborne?**
Michael Burke

118   **'Cars not casinos': the manufacturing revival**
Paul Everitt

131   **The entrepreneurial state**
Mariana Mazzucato

144   **'Managed' v 'market capitalism': the record**
Stewart Lansley

Editorial

Speaking for England

In this issue we continue discussion on a number of themes that are critical to rethinking left strategy and developing opposition to Coalition government policies - extending democracy across the regions and nations of the UK, a new welfare settlement, and a new political economy.

Our first three articles explore Englishness, regionalism and localism. As Paul Salveson argues, reconnecting with local and regional traditions of socialism is a crucial way of renewing left politics all around the country, as well as feeding into the national renewal that is so needed. And at the same time getting back in touch with local socialist traditions meshes naturally with the rethinking on Englishness that Anthony Painter is calling for. For it is in the regions that people are most likely to find their sense of place and identity.

All this points to the strong connections between issues of Englishness and democracy: and as Ken Spours argues, there is a socialist politics of localism that offers an alternative to New Labour's centralising tendencies while also rejecting the Tories' idea of a small (and therefore non-redistributive) central state. If we can revive a distinctive socialist take on local politics, at the same time as rethinking the distribution of decision-making between the centre and the regions, we will have gone along way towards beginning a national renewal of the left, while also making a major contribution to twenty-first century thinking on Englishness.

The next three articles continue our discussion on the public sphere, and in particular our efforts to alert readers to the massive withdrawal of support by the government for those living with incapacity or disability. Kaliya Franklin and Sue Marsh spell out this withdrawal in a frighteningly long list of benefits that the government is either reducing drastically or dropping all together. As they argue, at the same time as the government is urging the disabled to seek employment, it is taking away all the supports people need in order to be able to work. Declan Gaffney points out that neither the previous New Labour government nor the present

Editorial

Coalition seem to be able to come to terms with the idea that a normally functioning welfare state will always need to provide for people who are either temporarily out of work, or prevented from working by sickness or disability. As he demonstrates, current levels of incapacity benefit payments reflect the numbers of people living with incapacity. And yet on all sides we find resistance to looking after people in need disguising itself as a quest to weed out 'scroungers'.

This fundamental move away from a recognition that the state has an important role to play in looking after people is also affecting women disproportionately. As the Feminist Fightback Collective point out, the effect of draconian cuts across a whole range of services that contribute both to sustaining existing citizens and nurturing those of the future is to re-privatise women's work; and such an attempt to return to the good old-fashioned ways overlooks the fact that most women with children now also must have jobs outside the home, in order to be able to survive financially.

The last five articles continue the search for a new political economy. Andrea Westall argues that relational economics - which recognises that the economy is based in relationships, networks and connections - is a fruitful way of avoiding a one-size-fits-all mindset on the economy. As well as offering an important corrective to market fundamentalism, this is also an approach the left could usefully adopt. Michael Burke shows conclusively that shrinking the public sector is bad for the economy, since, as recent UK figures show, private investment follows on from public-sector-led recovery; as long as households and the government are not spending or borrowing to spend, the private sector is unlikely to invest in producing goods for them to buy. Paul Everitt puts the case for manufacturers: he hopes he detects in the government's rhetoric on manufacturing a recognition that the economy needs to rebalanced away from finance. Mariana Mazzucato discusses yet another area where dogma has prevented acknowledgement of the role of the state - the sphere of innovation, in which the large scale risk-taking that is required for major technological breakthroughs is almost never undertaken by private capital. Finally, Stewart Lansley demolishes the myth that free market capitalism has been good for the economy over the last thirty years, by showing that on almost all counts the post-war era of 'managed capitalism' outperforms the later period.

In the year ahead *Soundings* will be analysing and developing central themes in society, the economy and culture, to help create a Labour revival, and a new political strategy for the left.

Time for an optimistic Englishness

Anthony Painter

We need a new debate on Englishness.

National communities tend to be imagined or re-imagined at times of convulsive change and crisis. Yet though such change - social, economic, technological and constitutional - is currently undermining the political status quo, the English political conversation continues to be avoided. My argument here is that this avoidance is becoming increasingly unsustainable - and that a serious conversation on the issue is now overdue.

There are three potential sources that could force the English hand in this regard: an increasingly assertive and antagonistic English nationalism; a resurgent and forceful Scottish nationalism; and the changing contours of the international economy and financial crisis, which are likely to lead to constitutional change, especially - for our purposes here - within the EU and eurozone. And there are two dominant forms of evasion.

Sources of evasion

The first seeks to avoid rekindling *any* nationalism in a globalised, post-national world. But this liberal universalism has found it hard going in a post-9/11 world where security concerns and economic anxiety mesh: cultural antagonism has blended with economic insecurity to create nationally based resistance to the changes wrought by globalisation. Increasing labour mobility protectionism is just one example of this reactive impulse.

Time for an optimistic Englishness

But the stronger force for resisting a politics of Englishness is a status-quoism that wants to keep the Pandora's Box closed. The fear in this mind-set is that to open the dialogue is to take undue risk. In its conservative guise, the concern is the risk to the constitutional order: the argument seems to be that Englishness is a dormant identity that shouldn't be disturbed. In certain ways this is right. In British Social Attitude surveys over a number of years only one third of English respondents regard themselves to be English rather than British (though only a quarter favour British over English). The English want their own Parliament but are hardly mobilising with pitch-forks in order to secure one. And liberals and multiculturalists too have a voice in this risk-averse perspective. The fear is that antagonistic forces will take control of the dialogue, resulting in social and political disturbance. The fears are entirely understandable given the historical connectedness of nationalism, antagonism, racism and violence. As Paul Gilroy writes: 'The politics of "race" in this country is fired by conceptions of national belonging and homogeneity which not only blur the distinction between "race" and nation, but rely on that ambiguity for their effect'.[1] As Gilroy also notes, the Union Jack has now been replaced by the cross of St George as a threatening emblem of the far right. Englishness is replacing Britishness as the favoured form of exclusive identity. Contrastingly, only 14 per cent of Asians considered themselves English or 'hyphenated-English' rather than British in a recent survey that asked them to choose between these identities.[2]

The nub of the issue is whether a nation in mourning over its relative economic and geopolitical decline has the capacity for a generous dialogue about its English ethos: one that can find broad, inclusive and legitimate political expression. If the risks of initiating an Englishness dialogue are so great, why gamble? The answer is that there may be little other option.

Compelling reasons for discussion

England currently faces threats to its economic, cultural, and constitutional order both within and beyond its borders. The degree to which it is able to confront these threats will depend on a new political settlement.

Within its borders, the internal threat comes from an increasingly menacing expression of assertive and antagonistic monocultural nationalism. These forces take a number of forms: from violent street confrontation to nationalist populism.

Soundings

They mobilise around forms of English symbolic expression in a context of anxiety induced by economic change and dislocation, nostalgic loss of national pride, and significant cultural shifts. It is easy to dismiss the English Defence League simply as thuggery, or the British National Party as a rabble in respectable dress (interestingly, the party has suffered widespread defection to the *English* Democrats). But they represent something more sinister: a mutated nationalism in the absence of serious mainstream engagement with the natural desire for national belonging and meaning. This opens up the space for a rhetorical and angry lament of victimised alienation.

In 2010, the first man to be convicted under the Chemical Weapons Act 1996 was a white supremacist working with three other men. This has been largely ignored in the mainstream media. So the violent threat is real, but there is also a populist English nationalism that has yet to find mainstream political expression in the way that it has done in France, the Netherlands or Germany. And yet a similar widespread notion of cultural threat exists in England as in its European partners, as the Searchlight Educational Trust *Fear and Hope Report*, and other research, has demonstrated.

There are echoes here of the immigration debate, where mainstream political forces - particularly on the left - shied away from the issue in the early 2000s, only to find that by the time they arrived in the discussion the terms had already been set by the fearful tone of the right in media, popular and political discourse. Essentially, the mainstream emphasis has been on the more pluralist notion of Britishness - the good nationalism - while a political focus on Englishness has been largely avoided, leaving it as a cipher for more antagonistic political forces. But what then happens if Englishness is thrust centre-stage by external developments? There is enormous risk in mainstream political discourse trailing behind on this terrain.

Proceeding hand in hand and in intimate communion with antagonistic nationalism is the external threat of global economic change and crisis. The shift of the international division of labour towards emerging nations, and the economic muscle of those nations who enjoy a financial surplus, has had an impact on perceptions of identity. Taken at purchasing-power parity, the economic output of emerging economies overtook that of the OECD nations in 2008, and this has concentrated both the winners and the losers from global economic change within the UK.[3] And it is in the localities of loss, where economic change is most visible, that this process of identity reaction has been greatest; while the identity around

Time for an optimistic Englishness

which people have mobilised has increasingly been one of assertive Englishness.

There is also a constitutional ramification of global economic change that will increasingly impact on the UK's ability to maintain a flourishing economy amidst change. While the future of the eurozone is unclear, its survival is likely to depend on a new constitutional settlement between members, including some form of fiscal union. This will return the UK to a fringe position, with the main economic show being elsewhere - as it was prior to its signing of the Treaty of Rome in 1973. The concern is the degree to which this economic (self) exclusion will start to place England in an unfavourable position vis-à-vis neighbouring eurozone members, as they collude to stack the rules of game in their favour.

Over time, eurozone membership could become a more attractive proposition for Scotland if insider status becomes critical. This is one of the sources of threat to the continuance of the United Kingdom. If British economic and political union snaps, England could be left alone in its untended garden of antagonistic Englishness, facing unfavourable global economic change and constitutional change within the EU/eurozone. And even if independence and the eurozone do not prove to be sufficiently enticing alternatives to the UK for Scotland, any further devolution will place the politics of Englishness front and centre. Such change is a real possibility - and sooner rather than later.

Scotland's optimistic nationalism

Reformulations of national identity and major constitutional change have usually tended to be a response to some serious threat: security, cultural, or economic. The Act of Union in the early eighteenth century was such a response, as England sought to nullify ecclesiastical, dynastic and security threats from France and Catholicism, while Scotland sought to extract itself from an economic and financial hole. A similar period of political, civil and constitutional change occurred in the aftermath of the French revolution and Napoleonic wars. And Krishan Kumar notes that the first successful attempt at the formation of an English *nationalism* - though more cultural than political in form - was in the context of demands for Irish Home Rule and nationalist fervour on the continent at the end of the nineteenth and beginning of the twentieth centuries.[4]

It is less clear what threat motivates the current increasing success of Scottish

Soundings

nationalism as a political movement: Scottish nationalism is, it would appear, a nationalism of choice rather than necessity. Yet it has been remarkably successful, and this has significant consequences for England. John Curtice of Strathclyde University reports polling that shows 60 per cent of Scots in favour of either full independence (28 per cent) or so-called 'devo max' (32 per cent), whereby all powers are devolved to the Scottish Parliament other than those related to foreign policy, defence, and monetary policy. 'Devo max' is now a mainstream argument, and even received the backing of former prime minister John Major in a recent speech to the Ditchley Foundation:

> Why not devolve all responsibilities except foreign policy, defence and management of the economy? Why not let Scotland have wider tax-raising powers to pay for their policies and, in return, abolish the present block grant settlement, reduce Scottish representation in the Commons, and cut the legislative burden at Westminster?[5]

In a straight choice between separation and maintaining the status quo, it seems likely that the status quo would be maintained. But once 'devo max' is in the mix, things become significantly more complex, with the status quo becoming the second most likely option in any referendum. Furthermore, things may change over time - and rapidly. Another recent poll showed that support for independence was very strong amongst 18-34 year olds, and evenly split between 35-44 year olds; only those aged 44 and over are against.[6] Whatever happens in the Scottish government's proposed referendum, the current constitutional settlement seems an unstable one: a change of some sort is likely.

Scottish National Party leader Alex Salmond and his party have been able to construct a pluralistic and optimistic nationalism that fits Scottish society as it is, not as an idealised tartan utopia. At the 2011 opening of the newly-elected Scottish Parliament, Salmond evoked Robert the Bruce and William Wallace, but as voices of the *past* rather than of an Anglophobic present. Instead he reached for Scotland's twenty-first century voices: MSPs whose first language was Italian, Urdu and Arabic, alongside English, Gaelic, Scots and Doric. Scotland was to emerge from the 'glaur of self-doubt and negativity', no longer the junior partner but standing as an equal with England. This optimistic nationalism is about being better, whether it's a question of defeating alcohol abuse, building a new

Time for an optimistic Englishness

renewable-energy economy or confronting sectarianism.

If optimistic nationalism results in 'Devo max', it would create new English political institutions by default. New constitutional arrangements, a new economic challenge, and the sudden re-emergence of political Englishness would surely then focus the English political conversation. The internal threat of distorted Englishness, the global economic changes and constitutional change within a newly federal United Kingdom would combine to make the question of Englishness a mainstream and urgent political concern.

Paradoxically, Scottish nationalism is both a catalyst for this dialogue and also a guide as to how it can be managed while avoiding toxic overflow. Scottish nationalism's recent rise has been achieved without English people being beaten up in the streets, and without political vandalism or violence; though it aggressively and consistently challenges the constitutional order, it does so through democratic channels; and it presents a vision of the future rather than nostalgia or melancholy for the past. Scottish nationalism is not only a challenge to political Englishness; it could also chart its salvation.

Cultural liberty and national identity

There are, of course, limitations in adapting the optimistic nationalism pursued in Scotland to the conditions in England. Englishness and Britishness are proximate, and there is still an enormous commitment to the latter. The two terms are so close that they have often been used interchangeably - and this is perhaps one reason why the constitutional absurdities thrown up by devolution have largely been ignored.

Scotland has always been differentiated in some sense as a nation within the UK, even when this did not have political expression. As Arthur Herman has shown, Scotland was deliberately transformed intellectually, economically and culturally after the Act of Union.[7] This was a point of historical rupture. For England there was not a similar point of rupture after the union. There isn't a similar sense of an alternative view of national destiny that can be reached for; and nor do many English people contemplate the removal of the Stuarts from the throne in the Glorious Revolution (the most recent point of rupture in English history) with a sense of bittersweet regret. In contrast to this, many Scots mourn the end of independence in the context of national failure.

Soundings

Nonetheless there are clear elements of the Scottish approach which suggest a workable politics of national identity. It is non-culturally-deterministic, which enables it to respond to a pluralistic society. It is defined in its own terms, which avoids the pitfalls of creating a cultural 'other', to be differentiated or demonised. It is forward-looking, and so contains promise and avoids a debilitating politics of loss. Cultural liberty and national identity would seem to pull in opposite directions, but Scottish optimistic nationalism suggests that this need not necessarily be the case. It is possible to achieve an accommodation between the two.

In many ways, this approach to Scottish nationalism is compatible with the thinking of Amartya Sen, who rejects the notion of a singular and compulsory identity: 'The insistence, if only implicitly, on a choiceless singularity of human identity not only diminishes us all, it also makes the world much more flammable'.[8] For Sen the issue is choice: he is concerned about both communitarian monoculturalism and separatist multiculturalism (in effect 'plural monoculturalism'); and he quotes Gandhi's objection to groupist separatism as being the 'vivisection' of the Indian nation. It is possible for national identity to accommodate self-expression, as long as it does not take an acute form in which a sense of national coherence and togetherness can be lost.

In this context, a plural yet grounded national identity is but one aspect of an individual's identity, albeit one that has political consequences in a nation state - which is why Englishness is so politically contested. Two major strands, both of them unhelpful, have heretofore dominated the political discourse of Englishness - idealism and instrumentalism, as outlined below.

Contested Englishness

For Stanley Baldwin, Worcestershire-born Conservative prime minister of the 1920s and 1930s, Englishness was a sensibility:

> The sounds of England, the tinkle of the hammer on the anvil in the country smithy, the corncrake on a dewy morning, the sound of the scythe against the whetstone, and the sight of plough team coming over the brow of a hill, the sight that has been in England since England was a land … the one eternal sight of England.

Time for an optimistic Englishness

It is a beautifully constructed political speech. Unfortunately, it describes an England that no longer exists: there is no longer a tinkle of the hammer on the anvil; we don't hear the scythe on the whetstone; the corncrake is on the RSPB's red alert list, occasionally glimpsed only in western Scotland and Ireland; and the plough team is now mechanised - not so eternal after all (and already a very partial view of England in Baldwin's day). As evocative as Baldwin's speech was, it describes an England that we can only now access through the words and art of the past.

When Englishness assumes a monocultural form, when it is idealised and amplified, tightly defined and dissected, it quickly slips from grasp. Soon after, there is little option but to pursue an elegiac course and inevitably declare its death. Thus Conservative philosopher Roger Scruton has declared England dead - what else is there to do? His England includes parlour songs, the Saturday-night dance, the bandstand, and so on. And yes, those cultural forms and institutions have almost entirely gone.[9] Sir Roy Strong, in an iconographic account of England, locates Englishness - as an ideal - in rural traditions exemplified by landscape and social order. With breath-taking and unjustified boldness, he argues that this is the England we went to wars for: 'They [soldiers] did not fight for Manchester or Birmingham but for the likes of Chipping Camden and Lavenham'.[10]

Simon Heffer also sees England as 'monocultural' - though 'tolerant of other cultures'. No wonder there is such suspicion of Englishness amongst the many who don't feel that they fit into this monocultural straitjacket. A national identity with such an unbending attitude cannot hope to survive. And so England is declared dead, over and over again. And yet - Lazarus-like - it returns to life. Perhaps it is the universalising, idealised monoculturalism of a certain - admittedly often intoxicating - view of Englishness that needs to be rejected rather than Englishness itself.

Though often deploying similar techniques of belonging and loss, radical instrumental Englishness is usually framed as an alternative to this idealised monoculturalism. Alastair Bonnett has pointed to important sources of nostalgia in radicalism, and there is a recurring theme of returning home to a lost and uprooted existence.[11] Perhaps George Orwell's description of England as 'a family with the wrong members in control' encapsulates this perspective best, tied as it is to notions of 'home' that are intrinsic to nostalgia. Orwell was determined to separate patriotism from conservatism in his revolutionary Englishness. But this

Soundings

form of patriotism can quite quickly become instrumental, put to the service of a wider revolutionary mind-set. For Hobsbawm, patriotism must be fused with working-class interests. E.P. Thompson also, while rescuing Englishness for the English people, sees it as benign when put to the service of class interests.

Both these versions of Englishness - idealised and instrumental - fail to provide a viable pathway for an English political conversation. The first has little regard for the actual lives of English people as lived; the second is put to the service of some class interest and can only be justified in those terms. Both are unsatisfactory.

The work of Benedict Anderson always arises in discussions of national identity, and particularly his formulation of nations as 'imagined communities'. But Anderson's theory points to the historical development of nations as being embedded in specific convergences of economy, culture and technology. And if technology and economic change are key factors in creating the context for new ideological forms, then what of our current technological and economic context?

Technological and economic changes are fragmenting and pluralising culture. These include the rise of the internet, social media, and cable and satellite television; and the growth of the service sector, the expansion of consumerism and the decline of the large-scale employer and single-industry town. Social change is also contributing to this fragmentation, for example the increasing privatisation of community life, changes in family structure and power relations between men and women, historically significant migration flows, the diversity of popular culture, and the secularisation/religious diversification of spiritual life. The notion of the existence of a homogeneous working class - or any other historical agent for that matter - ready to be mobilised for revolution, seems fanciful in this technological and socio-economic world. Mass events that have near-universal national appeal, such as the royal wedding, are notable because of their rarity.

So the question then becomes: are there any fixed points of commonality? For without fixed points Englishness is likely to become a weak and divided plurality of monocultures. It is not at all clear that any national identity, other than a thin one of passport, flag and sports allegiance, could hold us together without thicker points of reference. There are notions of Englishness that have fixed form, including the primacy of the English language and the rule of law and the common law, supplemented by democratic statute. There also exists an affinity for the land - both rural and urban landscapes - and an aversion to extremes, which some argue can be seen in the Book

Time for an optimistic Englishness

of Common Prayer, and in English political history. But beyond these fixed notions there is a constant antagonism between different aspects of our national sensibility that is never resolved: little England v global citizen; north v south; radical v conservative; rural v urban; scientific v humanistic; and modern v traditional.

Englishness has elements that are sturdy, but also elements that are in perpetual tension. Some English cultural forms combine elements of fixedness and fluidity. There is a body of literature and art that is seen as a repository of commonly valued works of English iconography, and there is also an ever-changing and diverse body of new and newly discovered work. A set of historical stories enmeshes with a global history of nations and economic and intellectual development. Collective senses of memory and loss also include that of the migrant experience.

Fixed and contested - and beyond this fluid, plural and individual - notions of identity form a complex sense of modern Englishness. The challenge is to grasp all these components of national identity into something both real and imagined that can support a nation-state amidst internal and external change. To do so in a way that is meaningful and workable requires more than imagination; it requires political dialogue.

An English political dialogue

Scottish devolution was the outcome (but not the end point) of an inclusive civic process. By the time of the 1997 referendum, Scottish civil society was reconciled and positive about devolution. In other words, in contrast to referendums which have been defeated, such as that on AV and on the north-east assembly, civic dialogue led to constitutional change rather than vice versa. If the English question - how to politically reflect notions of Englishness - is to assert itself in a time of internal threat and external change, it is crucial to begin a dialogue immediately. But before dialogue can take place it is important to identify as dead ends both idealistic and instrumental Englishness. Neither permits a meaningful dialogue to take place, since their conclusions are predetermined. Equally, this exercise is not about rejuvenating an imperialistic missionary nationalism. That is another dead end that drags England back to a romanticised past. Instead the dialogue needs to be non-deterministic, pluralistic and democratic.

It will have a cultural element that will give voice to Englishness as actually

Soundings

experienced and felt, as both everyday practice and art (and the past is part of this story). It will have a civic element, as institutions of congregation and association on a local level and in new communities of interest are expressed as a relational Englishness (and there is much that is Burkean and Oakeshottian in this).

While Englishness is unlikely to be exclusive - the commitment to Britishness is deep - it will also be expressed in constitutional forms. Already there is an informal English legislative process: English laws, policies and regulations are passed in the Westminster parliament; it is just that non-English representatives vote on them too. If Scotland moves to 'devo max', this constitutional anomaly will be unsustainable. English parliamentary arrangements are likely to be necessary should devolution proceed any further - though they cannot simply take the form of the existing British institutions (of which many still remain), made English by a sleight of hand. Instead new institutions must fit the reality of English pluralism - an English Parliament for the English people as they are - not as we feel they should be, or once were.

Commitment to a national identity can move beyond cultural, civic and constitutional. There is also the promise of national identity - the 'American dream', Bismarck's corporate state, the extension and universalisation of the British welfare state after World War Two - all were, in Oakeshottian terms, 'enterprise' projects designed to underpin a sense of common citizenship. This substantive offer cannot be sidelined in any discussion about English political expression.

The demise of the corncrake, parlour games, and the forward march of the English working class may be regrettable but Englishness lives on. It appears to die and yet is continually re-born. This death and re-birth is traumatic. In the face of an alternative that is corrosive and antagonistic, and includes a threatening undercurrent of assertive Englishness, there can be no waiting for others to decide the English national fate. A constitutional, cultural, civic and citizenship-centred dialogue about Englishness becomes necessary. Paradoxically, such a dialogue could lead to a more settled and balanced federal United Kingdom. At the very least it should prise Englishness away from those who wish to use it to exclude and harm.

Anthony Painter is a political researcher, writer and commentator. He recently co-authored the *Fear and Hope* report and writes on the politics of identity and political change.

Time for an optimistic Englishness

Notes

1. Paul Gilroy, *There ain't no black in the Union Jack*, 2002 edition, p44.

2. Nick Lowles and Anthony Painter, *Searchlight Educational Trust Fear and Hope Report*, 2011.

3. *The Economist, Why the tail wags the dog*, 6-12 August 2011.

4. Krishan Kumar, *The making of English national identity*, 2003.

5. www.bbc.co.uk/news/uk-14093640.

6. www.politicshome.com/uk/article/29601/scots_independence_surge_backs_up_salmonds_strategy.html.

7. Arthur Herman, *The Scottish Enlightenment: the Scots' invention of the modern world*, 2001.

8. Amartya Sen, *Identity and violence: the illusion of destiny*, 2006.

9. Roger Scruton, *England: an elegy*, 2006.

10. Roy Strong, *Visions of England*, 2011, p10.

11. Alastair Bonnett, *Left in the past: radicalism and the politics of nostalgia*, 2010.

English socialism - regional accent?

Paul Salveson

Drawing on the many rich traditions that still exist within the regions and nations of Britain is a potential pathway to a renewed socialism nationally.

———

One of the most important fissures in the history of British socialism has been between its centralist and decentralist traditions, which cut across both the 'Marxist left' and 'social democratic right' (a more traditional counter-position, but one which is less salient for the purposes of my argument here). The decentralist tradition has its origins in the Painite radicalism of the late eighteenth century, and runs through Chartism, radical Liberalism, anarchism and the Co-operative movement; it has always sat uneasily within the Labour Party, but today it represents its best chance of re-emerging as a popular democratic force. To embrace this tradition, as well as other elements of the values-driven socialism which emerged across industrial Britain in the 1890s, requires a qualitative leap away from both the neoliberalism of Blair and the engrained authoritarianism of much of the left. The rich socialist traditions that still exist within the regions and nations of Britain offer an invaluable resource for those of us who want to embark on such a project.

North and South: A different kind of socialism

The roots of modern British socialism lie in the factories, railway depots and mines of Northern England, South Wales and the central belt of Scotland. The influence

English socialism - regional accent?

of the 'great men' - Fabians and middle-class individuals such as H.M. Hyndman and William Morris - has frequently been greatly exaggerated in accounts of the development of the left, and this ahs been to the detriment of more local and regional influences.

The Independent Labour Party was established in Bradford in 1893, and formed the political basis of the modern Labour Party. The choice of location was not accidental: the majority of delegates at the founding conference came from organisations based in Yorkshire and Lancashire. The ILP was a child of the industrial North. As E.P. Thompson has argued, fulminating against London-centric history:

> the ILP grew from the bottom up; its birthplaces were in those shadowy parts known as 'the provinces' … Its first council seat was won in the Colne Valley; its first authentic parliamentary challenges came in Bradford and Halifax: its first conference showed an enormous preponderance of strength in the North of England.[1]

In the years before the First World War, the difference between a 'Northern' ethical socialism that placed most stress on moral values, and the more Marxist-inclined London-based politics of the Social Democratic Federation, were apparent to several commentators. In 1895, Robert Blatchford, that flawed genius of socialist proselytising, wrote:

> … if you asked a London Socialist for the origin of the new movement he would refer you to Karl Marx and other German Socialists. But so far as our Northern people are concerned I am convinced that beyond the mere outline of State Socialism Karl Marx and his countrymen have had but little influence. No; the new movement here, the new religion, which is Socialism, and something more than Socialism, is the result of the labours of Darwin, Carlyle, Ruskin, Dickens, Thoreau and Walt Whitman.[2]

Martin Pugh corroborates this sense of difference, noting the immense variations in local political culture in the nineteenth century:

Soundings

> The inevitable result was a patchy geographical advance during
> Labour's early history and a movement that acquired pronounced
> local and regional characteristics ... Labour was not the same party in
> London as it was in Yorkshire ...³

Does any of this matter? I would argue it does. If socialism is to regain popularity, part of its appeal must lie in its being part of the fabric of locality, region and nation. There is much in our socialist heritage which - though almost buried - has relevance to modern-day politics, not least its stress on culture, 'values' and the importance of place.

The contours of early Northern socialism

The socialism that emerged in the North during the 1890s had roots not only in the radical Liberalism of the previous generation, but in the traditions of the handloom weavers of Pennine Lancashire and Yorkshire a century before. Many were radical democrats inspired by revolutionary France and the writings of Tom Paine. They had a highly developed culture, reflected in music, poetry, botany and natural science. That culture had been undermined by the ravages of industrial capitalism by the time of the Napoleonic Wars, and the Luddite revolts in 1812 were a desperate attempt to protect not only living standards but a whole way of life. By the 1830s handloom weaving was a dying trade, with tens of thousands thrown into poverty. Some of the weavers - and particularly their children - were forced to take work in the factories, and some of that culture and political radicalism went with them, exploding into Chartism not long afterwards. The life of Rochdale Chartist Tom Livsey was not untypical; Livsey moved from Owenite Socialism through Chartism to Co-operation and radical Liberalism in the 1850s.

That radical culture was not entirely forgotten in the late 1880s 'socialist revival'. In many towns of Lancashire and Yorkshire the surviving 'old Chartists' were venerated by the resurgent left in the Independent Labour Party. Socialists like Allen Clarke of Bolton wrote extensively about the great mass movements of the 1840s, in both fiction and journalism. The 'new socialism' sweeping the industrial North in the late 1880s and early 1890s understood who its predecessors were, and recognised the crucial importance of the Chartists' democratic agenda, as well as their social objectives.

English socialism - regional accent?

During this period, from the late 1880s up to the First World War, the North of England nurtured a crop of remarkable socialist visionaries. The work of Edward Carpenter has been recently 'rediscovered', thanks to the efforts of Sheila Rowbotham, but that of Allen Clarke, Caroline Martyn, Victor Grayson, Ethel Carnie, Katharine Bruce Glasier and Robert Blatchford remains virtually forgotten.[4] Blatchford's observation that Walt Whitman, Ruskin and other 'radical conservatives' such as Carlyle had had a greater influence on northern socialism than Marx have a great degree of truth. But there was also a degree to which the new socialism was internally-driven, taking some of the trappings of Nonconformity and weaving it into a distinctly northern socialist cloth.

By the end of the nineteenth century, the distinctive 'Northern' socialism that Blatchford had identified was firmly rooted in the textile districts of Lancashire and Yorkshire, and in the mining communities of the North East. It was strongly 'values' based, stressing community and fairness, opposition to child labour, a hatred of war, gender equality, socialisation of industry, and a love and respect for the countryside. It had a strong vein of working-class individualism, cultivated in the weaving communities of the Pennines, with their strong tradition of independence and self-help. It was community-based, but at the same time, internationalist. It was common for socialists in parts of Lancashire and Yorkshire to name their children after international heroes; Colne Valley ILP had an activist who rejoiced in the name of 'Kossuth Pogson'! There was a strong 'cultural' strand running through it, expressed in the flowering of socialist clubs, choirs, Clarion cycling and rambling clubs and debating societies. There was poetry in it; the locally rooted dialect of Allen Clarke, Ben Turner and Joseph Burgess, but also the mysticism and earthy sensual joy of Whitman. It also had a profoundly spiritual side, ranging from the orthodox religion of Nonconformity and Anglicanism through to Spiritualism and Whitmanite mysticism. The Labour Church movement, particularly strong in the North, was a rather clumsy attempt to bring 'God' and the labour movement closer together.

But one side of this socialism was highly practical; the work of the ILP's municipal pioneers had nothing 'woolly' about it, and led to very direct improvements in local health, child care, municipal transport and education. Fred Jowett of Bradford was the most well-known municipal socialist, but each town had its equivalent.

Soundings

What happened to this tradition? The ethical socialism of the ILP gradually gave way to a more calculating, narrowly parliamentary form of socialism. The First World War literally killed off many of its supporters, whilst some of the most radical elements of the left joined the Communist Party of Great Britain, which had little time for national, let alone regional, distinctiveness. The hard realities of government during the depression put enormous strain on the party, which eventually led to the collapse of the second Labour government in 1931, and the loss of two of its most talented, if controversial, leaders - Ramsay Macdonald and Philip Snowden. The ILP formally withdrew from the Labour Party in the following year.

It would be wrong to say that all traces of ethical socialism disappeared. The ILP in the North continued to publish *Labour's Northern Voice*, which carried regular features by Katharine Bruce Glasier, who did much to keep the flame alive. And the co-operative movement continued to provide an alternative focus for working-class political and social activity, as did the unions, though their strength was sapped by unemployment and anti-union legislation following the general strike of 1926.

The Labour landslide in 1945 was part of a remarkable, but short-lived, resurgence in socialist self-confidence. We need to dig a lot deeper into what happened across Britain at that time, and into the ferment of ideas which swept the Labour Party, unions and the Co-op in those few years, which was much more complex than is usually conveyed by those who mine Labour history looking for clues. There was certainly no consensus on the 'Morrisonian' model of public ownership being the only option, and a genuinely locally-rooted politics remained present across the country. But this peaceful revolution had run out of steam by the late 1940s, and a technocratic, Fabian-style Labour Party led its supporters to electoral defeat in 1951, and into subsequent political oblivion throughout the post-war years of rising prosperity. 'Labourism' became narrow, centralist and authoritarian, consciously rejecting the alternative co-operative tradition.

The importance of place and heritage

A new left emerged in the late 1960s, highly critical of Labourism. It was strong on some aspects of identity - gender, race and sexuality - but failed to recognise that locality and region had much greater potential in mobilising broad support. Labour had by this time become much too eager to ride roughshod over traditional

English socialism - regional accent?

identities, supporting Tory-led local government re-organisation, which not only destroyed historic county and town political identities, but also removed political power from the local level into amorphous new districts without any coherent identity. The political 'common sense' of the day, shared by much of the left and right, was a modernist cynicism that was comfortable with the destruction of entire communities in the name of 'slum clearance', the erection of tower blocks, the eradication of local identities, the closure of railways, and the idolisation of the emerging 'car culture'. Looking at each of those talismans of 1960s 'progress', few would doubt that this was fool's gold.

Many people, way beyond the Labour Party and left, value local culture and recognise the importance of 'place', including a sizeable body of 'one-nation' Tories. This is expressed on many levels. Membership of bodies like the National Trust and RSPB is at an all-time high, numbering millions. Local history continues to be immensely popular, with an ever-growing range of local festivals. People care passionately about their countryside - not just the national parks and areas of outstanding natural beauty, but the green lands adjoining urban communities which are facing major challenges from developers. Socialists need to stand with their communities in opposing a new rush of development which will ruin the character of thousands of local communities and destroy both local and regional distinctiveness: part of what adds up to 'England' (and all this is of course also true in the other nations of Great Britain).

For many, the idea of 'England' is in fact really 'the south'. Jeremy Paxman, in his highly entertaining book *The English: portrait of a people*, makes the point that when it comes to the idealised image of the nation: 'you could probably rule out anywhere north of a line from the Severn to the Trent. For not only is this imagined England rural rather than urban, it is southern rather than northern'.[5] This idea of England is incredibly powerful, and fundamentally reactionary and elitist. As Paxman notes, it offers nothing to the North - particularly its urban towns and cities. An alternative vision for England has to recognise and celebrate its cultural and geographical diversity - and that should find political expression in regionalisation.

The countryside has long been a 'political' issue, and in the North this found one form of expression in the mass trespasses such as those at Winter Hill, Bolton in 1896 and Kinder Scout in 1932. These showed how passionately working-class people in the North felt about their countryside: its defence was a profoundly unifying cause, stretching across classes and geography.[6] And although the fight for access to much of the countryside has been won, there are still some areas of land barred to the public, while there is every chance that more threats will emerge. The first big victory against the Coalition government in 2011 was their u-turn on the sale of woodlands. This was a real mass campaign, strongly supported by Labour but going well beyond the traditional anti-Tory lobby. It demonstrated clearly that people's love of the countryside can be mobilised in directly political ways; and that it is as much a concern to town-dwellers as to people in rural communities, if not more.

There is growing concern about the Coalition government's determination to relax planning restrictions and turn Britain into the sort of free-for-all which has blighted Ireland and much of the United States. We need to focus on the idea of distinctive self-sustaining communities, which can gain inspiration from the 'transition towns' movement and the growing mutual sector.

The environmental agenda ought to be one of socialism's strongest cards, and this is an area where we should make common cause with the Greens, instead of accusing them of being 'unrealistic'. Back in the 1890s Allen Clarke was pointing out the enormous damage to people's lives caused by unregulated industrial capitalism. The pollution from belching factory chimneys was seen by many at the time as 'natural', in much the same way we tend to regard car-borne pollution as a price we have to pay for mobility today.

Regional democracy

Keir Hardie and many of his comrades believed in 'Home Rule all round' for the UK as it then was, including England, Ireland, Scotland and Wales. The idea of English regional devolution, however, took many decades more to surface. Before the First World War, the North was a strong economic and political force with powerful local government; regionalism had little reason to exist. Certainly there was a very strong regional cultural consciousness, reflected in the popular dialect literature of Lancashire, Yorkshire and the North East, which to some extent cut across class divisions. But it did not translate into an overtly political consciousness that demanded devolved power from the centre.

It's different now. The economic gulf between north and south is widening and will get worse as Coalition cuts continue to have a disproportionate impact on the

English socialism - regional accent?

North. The economic and political power that was concentrated on Manchester, Liverpool, Leeds, Sheffield and Newcastle has gone. The industries which bolstered the strong city governments no longer exist and political power is in London. The revival of the North will not happen through benign centralist policies devised in Whitehall. A devolved, ethical socialism requires political expression at a regional level. The UK has already taken some significant steps towards devolution, in Scotland, Wales and Northern Ireland, and London has its own assembly with substantial powers, yet the rest of England has actually lost any vestige of regional power since the Coalition government came to power. The answer is not, as some argue, to have an 'English Parliament' - which would just be a 'London' Parliament - but to devolve power to the regions. Playing with English nationalism is inherently risky and will pull to the right.

In an English context, regionalisation is the best way to build a democratic, inclusive and vibrant nation, using states like Spain and Germany as positive examples. As Robert Putnam has argued in discussing the Italian regions:

> ... the regions characterised by civic involvement in the late twentieth century are almost precisely the same regions where cooperatives and cultural associations and mutual aid societies were most abundant in the nineteenth century, and where neighbourhood associations and religious confraternities and guilds had contributed to the flourishing communal republics of the twelfth century. And although these civic regions were not advanced economically a century ago, they have steadily outpaced the less civic regions both in economic performance (at least since the advent of regional government) and in quality of government.[7]

All the experience of regional government in continental Europe suggests that it can have a transformative effect, providing it is directly elected and takes power away from the centre. The experience in Scotland and London shows that devolution can bring vastly improved services, including new railways and infrastructure; and the 'clear red water' which separates Wales from England is now becoming deeper, with a Welsh Assembly Government increasingly confident of its power and independence following the 2011 referendum on gaining greater powers.

Soundings

John Prescott, a politician far too easily (and perhaps snobbishly) dismissed, had well-formed ideas for democratic regionalism, but they were less than enthusiastically championed by Blair. The 2004 referendum on devolution for the North East seemed almost specifically designed to go against the government: little power was to be devolved to the proposed regional assembly, and there was a strong sense that it would simply become another tier of bureaucracy. The solution which followed this debacle - to have unelected 'city region' governments covering smaller areas - was a classic compromise, and with a serious democratic deficit. 'City regions' are just too small. All the development over the last thirty years has been for the economy and the transport system to outgrow cities or even city regions. People travel ever longer distances into work, and supply chains become bigger and bigger. People's leisure and work patterns have extended over much longer distances, bringing the city and countryside into much closer contact. A 'city region' that excludes its rural hinterland will result in unbalanced development, and a countryside which is little more than a playground for the rich.

Building strong regional government

The need for a new form of regional government will sooner or later re-assert itself. Labour, working with allies amongst the Greens and Liberal Democrats, should develop a new regionalism within England that is democratic, inclusive and with real clout, taking power away from the centre rather than the locality. It is regional government, mobilising civic power through a network of mutual enterprises, which stands the best hope of reviving the flagging economies of the North, not some fanciful 'trickle-down' of wealth from the South-East.

Transport is a key area where a regional centre-left approach is needed. The early pioneers of the ILP wanted a publicly owned rail system and municipally owned trams and buses. Today, a sustainable transport policy should be delivered by well resourced regional transport agencies, accountable to directly elected regional assemblies. These agencies should determine the shape of an integrated public transport network, making the most of rail, bus and tram. New forms of social ownership need to be applied to the national rail network, including train-operating companies being structured as co-operatives, or being taken into ownership by the regions as arms-length public companies. The huge semi-monopolies controlling

English socialism - regional accent?

Britain's bus operations also need to be reformed, with encouragement to smaller, mutually and/or municipally owned operators.

A modern centre-left regionalism needs to address ways of making new regional government part of a wider democratic revolution. As we have noted, part of the reason that the referendum on North East devolution failed was the limited powers to be devolved to the proposed assembly and the sense that it would be 'more of the same old stuff'. England has become less, not more democratic in the last few years, and it's time to start a debate on how a new England, within a federal UK, should look.

Labour and its allies need to work out a radical plan for local and regional government which learns from best practice abroad. A central lesson is that it must be democratically elected, rather than being a jumble of indirectly-elected councillors and unelected business people and local worthies. Austin Mitchell, the quirky but perceptive MP for Grimsby, summed up the issues as far back as 1989:

> Proportional representation - representing the people's wish in parliament - should be the central part of a wider process; entrenching rights, in the constitution, at work, to services, as citizens: decentralisation of power by breaking down the dominance of The Great Wen and establishing regional governments, not only in Scotland and Wales but in all the English regions with powers transferred down from the centre and up from the counties ...[8]

Alongside the need for strong regional government and a fairer electoral system, the case needs to be made for a root and branch reform of how government actually functions. If regional government is seen as just another attempt at creating jobs for the (mostly male) political class it will fail. It's time to breathe new life into British politics, and a big part of that is widening the pool of talent for councillors and MPs. Class needs to re-emerge alongside gender, sexuality and race as an area of political concern.

Within the left, we should do more to celebrate, but also to understand, the heritage which is distinctly ours, through events such as Bolton's Whitman Day, Wigan's 'Digger' commemoration, the Tolpuddle Festival and Halifax Chartist Festival. This is not about turning socialism into a heritage theme park; there is a need to link our histories with people's current identities and concerns. The left needs to develop a diverse identity which can celebrate the memory of the Peterloo martyrs, the achievements of the women's suffrage campaigners, and municipal socialists and the early co-operators, whilst reaching out to every section of communities as they are today, celebrating and safeguarding a strong sense of place and identity.

Conclusion

Labour cannot win national elections if it is just seen as the 'Northern Party', and nothing in this article should suggest that it ought to retreat into its geographical comfort zones. It needs to connect with people's Northern identities, but also with their Welsh, Scots, East Anglian, Cornish, London and other identities. This is a cultural as much as an economic issue. It is not about trying to breathe life into an out-dated cloth-cap idea of 'northern-ness' that potentially excludes the array of 'new' communities that are now firmly established in many regions.

If socialism is to have any relevance in the twenty-first century it must be de-centralised, community-based and diverse - and with a sense of humour. Can Labour recapture some of the radicalism and passion which informed the early years of the ILP and the Clarion movement over a hundred years ago? It needs to rediscover ways of working as a party which take us out of the committee room and into communities and workplaces.

The right has been in the intellectual ascendancy for far too long. A new centre-left should have the self confidence to challenge both Blairite neoliberalism and Thatcherite Conservatism, whilst recognising potential allies in other political traditions - including radical Liberalism and one-nation Toryism. The politics of place and the countryside are two areas where the left could come to occupy a hegemonic position. Labour should take the initiative in setting up pilot 'regional commissions' across England. A twenty-first century 'Council of the North' that is truly representative of the communities and interests which make up the North could develop a radical programme not just for regional governance but for the economic transformation of the region.

The early ILP was by definition an immature movement, and the realities of office in the 1920s led to a retreat from the fun and tomfoolery, as well as the quasi-

English socialism - regional accent?

religious appeals, of the early days. But there are things we can learn from those times, finding ways of reconnecting with people's lives and culture in the widest sense, so that socialism can re-build itself as a popular force across an increasingly diverse Britain. We need to redefine in a modern context that 'ethical socialism' of the North, building the foundations of a decentralist, values-based socialism that has the potential to inspire people today. It doesn't mean turning one's back on 'England'; it means creating a democratic and inclusive nation that can celebrate its regional diversity as well as its shared achievements, together with the other nations of Britain.

Paul Salveson is a professional railwayman and visiting professor at the University of Huddersfield. He originated and developed the 'community rail' concept and was awarded an MBE 'for services to the railway industry' in 2008. He is vice-chair of Colne Valley Labour Party and active in his union TSSA. His book *Socialism with a Northern Accent* will be published by Lawrence and Wishart later this year. His most recent book was *Allen Clarke/Teddy Ashton: Lancashire's Romantic Radical* (Little Northern Books 2009).

www.paulsalveson.org.uk

Notes

1. E.P. Thompson, 'Homage to Tom Maguire', in John Saville (ed.), *Essays in Labour History* 1972.

2. Robert Blatchford, 'The New Party in the North', in Reid (ed.), *The New Party*, 1895.

3. Martin Pugh, *Speak for Britain: a new history of the Labour Party*, 2010.

4. Sheila Rowbotham, *Edward Carpenter: a life of love and liberty*, 2009; Paul Salveson, *Allen Clarke/Teddy Ashton: Lancashire's Romantic Radical*, 2009; for the influence of Whitman and his English followers, including Katharine Bruce Glasier, see Paul Salveson, *With Walt Whitman in Bolton: spirituality, sex and Socialism in a Northern Mill Town*, 2008.

5. Jeremy Paxman, *The English: portrait of a people*, 1998.

Soundings

6. The Winter Hill Trespass was much bigger than Kinder, but less documented. See Paul Salveson, *Will Yo' Come O' Sunday Mornin'? The Winter Hill Trespass of 1896*, 1996.

7. R. Putnam, 'Federalism, Regionalism and Planning', in Putnam et al, *Making Democracy Work: civic traditions in modern Italy*, 1993.

8. *Britain: Beyond the Blue Horizon*, 1989.

SOCIALISM
WITH A NORTHERN ACCENT
Radical traditions for modern times

Paul Salveson

In this new book – which is so much more than a work of history – Paul Salveson re-asserts the strength and distinctiveness of the socialism which emerged in the mills, mines and railway yards of the North of England. He argues that popular socialism today needs to reconnect with its local and regional roots. Central to this account is an examination of the Independent Labour Party, formed in Bradford in 1893, which emphasised ethical values, community and culture, and Salveson shows how the co-operative movement and the trades unions, alongside the ILP, helped shape a durable and independent working-class culture.

As Salveson argues, in reconnecting with these local radical traditions in a modern context Labour could find valuable resources for its renewal.

Paul Salveson is a professional railwayman and visiting professor at the University of Huddersfield. He was awarded an MBE for services to the railway industry in 2008 and is vice-chair of Colne Valley Labour Party. He has written widely on labour in the North, including *Allen Clarke/Teddy Ashton: Lancashire's Romantic Radical* (Little Northern Books, 2009).

SPECIAL OFFER
Buy online now for just £11.99 (plus p&p) and save £3
www.lwbooks.co.uk

Democratic localism

Ken Spours

Some on the left see only two versions of localism, but we need to discover a third.

———

The issue of localism is often a difficult one for some on the left, as they find themselves caught between support for a socialist, distributive and egalitarian central state and support for devolution and greater democracy. The disagreement between the 'centralisers' and the 'democrats' has usually seen the first dominate the second, and the left has gained a historical reputation for governmental centralism and weak democratic intent. Soviet state socialism represented the anti-democratic tendency in the extreme, and western social democracy, while having extended the franchise and the welfare state, exhibited a tendency towards elitism and suspicion of mass participation. New Labour perpetuated this tradition, because its political focus on managerial control and market-based choice was far greater than its commitment to greater local control and democratic participation in public services. A 'democratic hesitancy', reflected in different ways across most of the left, has thus provided acres of political space for the right to cast themselves as the new democrats who will pioneer the freedom of the people. This is the immediate political significance of debates about localism in the English context.

The left's confused and reactive stance has profound consequences, not only because of the political space it vacates to the right, but because it is evidence of a failure to understand the relationship between achieving greater democracy and greater fairness. Moreover, the 'left centralisers' have treated localism as if it is a single political phenomenon, seeing only its neoliberal variants. They fear, with some justification, that greater inequalities will result from more power being exercised at a local level, because of the retreat by central government from an equity

Democratic localism

role. Closer scrutiny suggests, however, that instead of seeing only two - neoliberal - variants of localism, it is time to discover another. My argument is that a third version has appeared over the past decade - the 'new localism' - that offers a basis from which a full democratic model can be developed.

The crisis of governance and democracy

The political interest in localism currently being shown by all the main political parties is partly a response to a deep and accumulating crisis of governance and democracy. After three decades of neoliberalism there has been an increasing crisis of political legitimacy, as people have become less deferential, while at the same time fearing insecurity and the lack of control over important aspects of their lives. In this 'post-democratic' situation, strong markets have dominated and increasingly controlled weak democracies. Furthermore, greater consumer choice has been accompanied by the erosion of political choice, as the main political parties have converged on centre ground and the right has repeatedly attacked the capacity of the state to be able to offer solutions to the crises that arrive with increasing rapidity.[1]

This crisis of governance and democracy has taken on a particularly acute form in the UK (or more accurately England), and New Labour has to share a large part of the blame for the breakdown in trust between the people and government. The popular hope invested in New Labour in May 1997 was squandered, particularly from the period from 2003 onwards, with the war in Iraq, 'high Blairism', the politics of spin, the building of a 'data-base state' and, eventually, the inability of Gordon Brown to signal a departure from New Labour's managerialism. It was this growing climate of authoritarianism that helped nourish the Conservatives' concept of the 'Big Society' and its version of localism. But the crisis was not only of New Labour's making; it had deeper neoliberal roots - the banking crash, the MPs' expenses scandal, the new government's austerity measures that go beyond manifesto commitments, the newspaper hacking scandal, and the recent riots in English cities - all these suggest that the relationship between people and state is further eroding. Through the different phases of this crisis, political parties have been trying to reconnect with the people through the prisms of their own ideologies. It is from this process that different versions of localism, the state and democracy have emerged.

Soundings

Three versions of localism

Disagreement within the left about localism reflects a wider debate within the research community about the role of national government in the delivery of public services, and about the nature of governance. Here, discussion has largely centred on how national governments can respond to the pressures of globalisation and technological change, and to the increasing complexities they face in terms of the composition and organisation of societies, as well as the existence of problems that cannot be solved at national government level. While there is little disagreement about the emergence of new forms of governance, there are differences about their significance and benefits. Some argue that 'the revival of the local' is nothing less than a neoliberal means of assisting markets to become more efficient, less regulated by national governments and potentially exclusionary; for others the idea heralds a new era of popular participation in shaping localities and public services.[2]

This is not simply an English issue, although it has particular resonances in the English political environment because of the degree of centralism of our political system. Promoting the local has become the vogue, and all the main political parties are 'gargling with localism at the moment', as they seek to promote a more responsive approach to the delivery of public services.[3] While their approaches to localism share certain features, they differ primarily about the role of the state in shaping public services, and in the different emphases they place on the respective roles of national, regional and local government, and of markets and democratic participation.

Three different versions of localism can be traced through the debates and policies in the English context over the past ten years. The first is associated with the previous Labour government, whose attempts at empowering the local were very much subordinate to its centralist drive to reform public services. The second version has emerged from the Coalition government, whose ideas of local empowerment are closely tied to its notion of a smaller central state and a larger role for markets and privatisation. A third - and more fruitful - version can be associated with what has been termed the 'new localism', which includes examples of policy developments in Scotland and Wales, where devolved administrations have been pursuing distinctive approaches to the governance

Democratic localism

of public services. This last version has the potential to be part of a wider process of democratising the state, whereas the previous two are simply different neoliberal variants.

New Labour's centrally managed localism and the politics of distrust

New Labour's version of localism was shaped by the twin strands of managerialism and a mild social democracy, part of what Stuart Hall referred to as its 'double shuffle' (see *Soundings* 43). In terms of the delivery of public services, the dominant strand was central steering, via national arms-length agencies and centrally devised policy levers - such as targets, performance measures, funding, inspection and national initiatives - together with the encouragement of competition between providers in a quasi-market. The subordinate strand comprised attempts to promote 'joined-up government' at national, regional and local levels (e.g. the Every Child Matters Agenda); to champion what was termed 'double devolution'; and to capture the 'user voice' at the point of delivery.[4] Citizen involvement, however, was very much related to promoting competition, efficiency and consumer satisfaction, rather than to the development of sustained democratic involvement in shaping services, as has been the case in Wales for example.

New Labour undertook a wide range of devolution initiatives. It met demands for the devolution of governmental powers to Scotland and Wales in 1999; it restored devolved government to Northern Ireland in 2007; and it experimented with regionalism. Lastly, it partially resurrected an integrating and commissioning role for local authorities, for example via single regeneration budgets, strategic area agreements and area-wide inspections. However, despite these initiatives it will be remembered more for its top-down managerialism and promotion of markets than for its attempts to devolve power. The critical moment for New Labour and localism came with the publication of the Lyons Report on Local Government in 2007, which recommended that ministers should 'give power away' and reform local government finances. Dubbed by many 'Tame Lyons', even this report proved too radical for ministers, and was promptly kicked into the political long grass. New Labour's centrally managed localism ultimately came to nothing, as its rule petered out amidst a series of economic and political crises.

Soundings

The Coalition, laissez-faire localism and the politics of a smaller state

The Coalition government's approach to localism can be seen, in part, as a political reaction to New Labour's authoritarianism, and as a critique of the role of a large and expensive centralised state. Its announcements so far, and its 'Localism and Communities Bill', suggest that it is actively promoting a new version of localism based on a reduced role for central government and the size of the state; an emphasis on institutional autonomy; and the encouragement of greater numbers of private and third sector providers within a competitive climate. This is linked to a rhetoric of empowering citizens and communities as consumers and active participants in public services, and the promotion of 'local markets' in areas such as health and education. It would appear that Cameron is engaged in his own double shuffle, in which the discourse of the Big Society connects ideas about a reduced state and an increased role for markets to community involvement and local democracy. This approach has been termed 'laissez-faire localism' because of its emphasis on the freeing up of communities and localities to pursue their own agendas within what appears to be another wave of privatisation and the contracting out of services - as seen for example in the 'Easy Council' concept of public services that is being promoted by local authorities such as Barnet and Suffolk. Its democratic intent has also to be seriously questioned, not least because of the diktats that have flowed from Coalition ministers, notably in the areas of education and local government.

Democratic localism and rebalancing the state

These two versions are part of the same neoliberal universe, insofar as each is both centralising and pro-market. However, a third version of localism, known as the 'new localism', has emerged over the past decade in the debates about democracy and the local delivery of services that have flourished in response to the dysfunctions and political unpopularity of the top-down managerialist approach to the governance of public services. Gerry Stoker eloquently summarised the aims of the new localism as:

> a strategy aimed at devolving power and resources away from central control and towards front-line managers, local democratic structures and local consumers and communities, within an agreed framework of

Democratic localism

> national minimum standards and policy priorities.[5]

This perspective finds wider support in research communities involved in the study of local government, and in the work of those associated with social-democratic and liberal politics in the UK; and it is practised, to a limited degree, by the devolved administrations in Wales and Scotland.

In contrast to the first two versions, this third variety of localism stresses not only popular participation at the lowest possible levels, but also a strong role for national government to provide frameworks to address issues such as wage inequality, inequity of access to public services and economic co-ordination. It also envisages distinctive roles for regional and local government, for example with regional formations providing co-ordination in areas such as skills and labour markets as part of a process of decentring power and control. There has been a particular interest in the balance between the national, regional and local levels of decision-making, and the role of communities and civil society organisations, both public and private, in the delivery of public services. This has also involved the recognition that regional and local levels of government are more established and active in several other European countries than in the UK, and particularly in England. My suggestion is that the concept of democratic localism can emerge out of the new localism if its devolution agenda can become part of a much wider strategy for democratisation from national to local and back again.

A new approach to leadership and the culture of national politics

Democratic localism is not just about reform at the bottom. Changes lower down require reform at the top. At the centre of this third version has to be a new democratic culture of national politics. This involves accepting that there are distinct but limited roles for national government, for example in developing a political narrative and direction of travel of policy; guaranteeing equity and universal entitlements; setting standards; and co-ordinating the economy. Part of this redistribution of decision-making will be a new form of leadership - moving away from micro-management and towards strategic leadership, and thus marking a decisive break with the previous culture of constant interference and endless national initiatives, in general tied to ministerial careers. This more deliberative and slower approach of politics requires nothing less than the democratisation of the centre. Such an approach can be seen as a way of 'saving representative democracy', and this re-organisation of the centre would include a greater role for parliament in policy-making, more free parliamentary votes, a greater focus on parliamentary deliberation and the Select Committee system, and, crucially, the development of a fairer national voting system.[6]

For localism to flourish, the process of democratisation requires the political courage to give power away, and to nurture the levels of governance below, safe in the knowledge that people on the ground will know their problems and their potential solutions better than many politicians. But how can we prevent this process of decentring from resulting in local fragmentation? Some have suggested that policy levers - which are the instruments of top-down governance (targets, funding, inspection and performance criteria) - should be replaced by 'policy frameworks', which provide the 'rules' and 'freedoms' to stimulate collective practice between social partners and encourage local innovation. Lawrence Pratchett usefully conceptualises this rebalancing by making a distinction between the autonomy of 'freedom from' higher authority and the responsibility of 'freedom to' act collectively and effectively at the regional and local levels.[7] Others have gone further, in arguing that in order to reap the rewards of efficiency, effectiveness, equity and greater democratic accountability, 'the legitimacy of local government as a tier of government should be constitutionally protected, as it is in other EU states'.[8]

A strong networked regional level

Is there a role for the region in a vision of localism? Not according to the Coalition government, which associates regionalism with an additional layer of bureaucracy. New Labour did try to develop regional co-ordination around skills development, but it failed to provide the regions with any real co-ordinating power, despite the existence of regional development agencies. Furthermore, it went about its regional strategy the wrong way round, thinking that the regions could follow the same trajectory as Scotland and Wales, and would be based on elected assemblies, rather than first demonstrating the usefulness of their role in co-ordination and strategic planning. That was stopped in its tracks by the 'No vote' in a referendum in the North East in 2004. Moreover, the previous government's own centralism also

Democratic localism

frustrated the real empowerment of the regions. In the end, New Labour's regional strategies were as (if not more) muted than its local ones.

But a democratic localist strategy will depend on a much more high-profile regional approach, one that is focused on the integration of the economy, skills and innovation. One example of good practice in this field are the strongly collaborative regional social partnerships - including employers, further and higher education and regeneration agencies - that have taken root in Australia (an Anglo-Saxon-type national system) around the concept of 'high skill eco-systems', which integrate employment, skills and specialised vocational education.[9] Moreover, and closer to home, a regional strategy will enable a confrontation of the real regional inequalities that are the result of the concentration of economic power in London and the South East. Reducing regional inequalities will also require a strong national industrial strategy to decentre the economy, built around 'needs-based' growth strategies. From the building of these economic and skills strategies and their support networks could flow demands for a greater civic voice and democratic representation, built around a non-parochial sense of regional belonging. Given the weakness of regions in the English political landscape, people may have to appreciate the added value of regional economic and skills co-ordination before they are prepared to agree to an additional tier of democratic governance.

Reinventing the local

Despite the political rhetoric from all major parties about devolving powers to local government and localities, the political and governance system in England remains highly centralised. New Labour offered local government a Catch-22. They would not devolve power until local government became more accountable and competent; leaving local government to claim that it could not become more accountable and competent without greater devolution. The Coalition, on the other hand, has promised to devolve powers to localities, but local government has seen billions of pounds stripped out of its budgets, and the only devolution it appears to be experiencing is that of making painful decisions about cutting services within the new regime of austerity. The steady erosion of the legitimacy of local government and its capacities to act creatively by successive governments (despite areas of notable innovation) has reduced its public popularity, with low voting turnouts in local elections reflecting this.

Local government needs greater powers to shape the local landscape and to reconnect people. Someone has to 'dare more democracy'. Here is an opportunity for the left to focus on civic leadership; the direct involvement of communities in decision-making (for example through innovations such as 'citizen's juries', where problems are deliberated over time using expert witnesses); the co-production of public services; and participatory budget-making in local government. People do think the local is important, but they have to also believe that it can make a difference. The future of local government and governance is not linked solely to competence and the ability to bring about changes; it is intimately tied to the renewal of democracy at the local level, and this starts from the premise that localism is not just about what a council does for the people, but how the people are able to shape the world around them.

Expanding democracy - beyond statism and markets

Democratic localism is therefore not just about the local; it is about a rebalancing of relationships at different levels of the state and civil society - national, regional, local and community - within a much more explicitly public realm. In this sense, it is more democratic than local, because it only flourishes within a full democratising approach. This approach to change is not something alien to the left, but part of its history. It is worth reflecting on the founding traditions of the labour movement - the traditions of self-help, mutualism, co-operatives, friendly societies and trade unions, before the advent of statism. Democratic localism, drawing on this aspect of the past, could prove to be a unifier of social-democratic and liberal traditions in a broader democratic left.

How do we move from where we are now to where we might want to be? The three versions of localism presented here are ideal types, and are particular representations of approaches towards the state. In reality, features of all three may be found at any one moment, in parts of national government, and in specific areas of the public service sector or a given locality. The question is which of the three versions is dominant and shapes the others. Moreover, some credit also has to be given to the two versions of localism that I have taken issue with. Both have their democratic elements, but they remain subordinate to statist, centralising and market

Democratic localism

logics. Democratic localism is therefore not about creating an entirely new world; it is about strategically expanding democratic life wherever we see it.

Finally, I want to return to the apprehensions of the left centralisers. What force can hold together a democratising strategy at all levels of state and civil society so that the quest for greater local control does not result in greater social difference? It is the political party, working to connect the different levels of political activity within a strategic vision of transformation.[10] Localism has been debated for over ten years, but understanding the role of the party in this new context has hardly begun.

Ken Spours is a professor of education at the Institute of Education, University of London and convenor of the Compass Education Group.

Notes

1. For an analysis of the erosion of the democratic state see Neal Lawson, 'Rethinking the role of the state' in J. Rutherford and A. Lockey (eds) *Labour's future*, 2010: http://www.lwbooks.co.uk/ebooks/laboursfuture.html.

2. Arguments associating the new localism with new democratic opportunities include G. Stoker, *New Localism, Participation and Networked Community Governance*, University of Manchester 2004: www.ipeg.org.uk/papers/ngcnewloc.pdf. Arguments associating localism with neoliberalism include N. Brenner and N. Theodore, 'From the New Localism to the spaces of Neo-liberalism', in N. Brenner and N. Theodore (eds), *Spaces of neo-liberalism: urban restructuring in North America and Western Europe*, Blackwell and Ball 2002.

3. D. Boyle, *Localism: Unravelling the Supplicant State*, New Economics Foundation 2009.

4. Voices from the front bench of New Labour in favour of localism included speeches from Hazel Blears, 2005, and David Miliband, 'My New Year's Resolution for Local Government', *Localist*, Jan/Feb 2006.

5. See his *New Localism, Participation and Networked Community Governance*.

6. Neal Lawson, *Dare more democracy: From steam-age politics to democratic self-*

government, Compass 2005.

7. L. Pratchett, 'Local Autonomy, Local Democracy and the "New Localism"', *Political Studies* 52, 2, 2004.

8. E. Cox, *Five Foundations of Real Localism*, IPPR 2010, p9.

9. R. Hall and R. Lansbury, 'Skills in Australia: Towards Workforce Development and Sustainable Skill Ecosystems', *Journal of Industrial Relations* 48, 5, 2006.

10. This Gramscian concept of the political party, functioning as an 'organic intellectual', is discussed in a rigorous and accessible way in Anne Showstack Sassoon *Gramsci's Politics*, Croom Helm 1987.

The benefits scandal

Kaliya Franklin and Sue Marsh

The government is withdrawing the support that enables disabled people to work, while simultaneously arguing that more of them should be working.

———

Despite significant progress in earlier decades towards enshrining legal rights and protection for disabled people, beginning with Lord Morris's Chronically Sick and Disabled Person's Act (1970), the future of the disabled community now appears uncertain. The drive towards independent living, and efforts to establish rights to access businesses, services, transport, education and employment through the Disability Discrimination Act (now Equalities Act), are now being thwarted by the proposed cuts. Prior to the 2010 election the outlook was already stormy, in the context of rising hate crimes and the demonisation of welfare claimants by a slavering media egged on by politicians - with one eye firmly on the welfare balance sheet and the other determinedly closed to the consequences of their actions.1 Then, within months of their election, the Coalition government were championing and cheering on a round of cuts that are increasingly devastating in their impact upon disabled people. Because of this, a new generation of sick and disabled people have now been radicalised into activism.

Two perceptions of sickness and disability pervade mainstream thinking. On the one hand there are the lazy scrounging scum, perfectly able to work if they choose, draining resources from an already overburdened taxpayer; on the other there are the deserving claimants, pitiful creatures, who will be provided for with free cars, bungalows and holidays as compensation for their lot. Neither image reflects reality, but the former continues to be cemented in the public consciousness, fed by a diet of moral outrage based upon statistics that the DWP themselves have been forced to admit give a distorted picture.[2] As to the latter image - it is based on a misconception amongst the general public that, should they become sick or disabled, the state will step in and willingly provide all that is needed. The dominance of these contradictory and inaccurate ideas helps to explain why the savage cuts that are being championed in the name of reform are going largely unchallenged. It seems that, whilst most of the public can immediately understand the importance of saving forests for all our futures, an understanding of the importance of sickness and disability benefits and services tends to be confined to those who are directly affected.

However, the introduction of Disability Living Allowance (DLA) in 1992 was an acknowledgement that sickness and disability bring with them additional and unavoidable financial burdens. But Thatcher's drive towards community care during the 1980s - initially welcomed as a positive step by the disability rights movement - was never sufficiently funded, and this meant that part of the effect of the new DLA was to transfer to individuals funding that had previously gone to institutions, as people moved into independent living. Separated into two components, for mobility and care, DLA was an important part of the fledgling personalisation agenda. This perception has therefore always been something of a mixed blessing, but it did at least allow some people to live more independently.

Within months of their 1997 election victory New Labour had announced plans to dramatically curb eligibility to disability benefits, on the basis that spending had doubled and must be curbed. Charities greeted this announcement with outrage, and pointed to the legitimate reasons for the increases in costs, which were being ignored by government; these included medical advances, the costs of community care, and the success of efforts to encourage take-up of these benefits. One noteworthy protest involved people in wheelchairs chaining themselves to the Downing Street gates and throwing red paint around, to symbolise 'Blair's blood'.[3] Soon after, the first plans for reforming disability benefits were quietly shelved.

During the following decade a new generation of disabled people - born with an expectation of their right to live independently - began to come of age, and they were joined by larger numbers of people who had recently become sick and disabled in the course of their working, tax-paying lives. Together they constituted a generation who had not known the horror of imprisonment in institutions. Having lived more freely for a while, disabled people were at first slow to recognise the threats being made to their independence. However, New Labour had not

The benefits scandal

given up on their 'reforms' of welfare provision, and in October 2008, after a long period of preparing the ground, previous disability benefits were replaced by a new Employment Support Allowance (ESA), whose eligibility criteria seemed deliberately designed to exclude large numbers of people from benefits.

High unemployment throughout the 1980s had also undoubtedly contributed to the numbers of people claiming Incapacity Benefit (IB); this was because mostly male, older claimants, who were far more likely to have industrial injuries or sickness from their working years, had been deliberately directed towards incapacity benefit as a way of reducing unemployment figures.[4] But this group were then seized upon by politicians as characterising the entire claimant group, and were used to justify major efforts to reduce the number of IB claimants, in the first instance in measures put forward by John Hutton. Then, during Peter Hain's stewardship, the Department of Work and Pensions used research carried out at Cardiff University, part-funded by the American private insurance company Unum, to move towards a 'biopsychological' model of sickness and disability.[5] Deeply concerned by the rise in insurance claims for sickness and disability that lacked clear 'biological markers', the basic premise of the biopsychosocial model was to reclassify the concept of sickness preventing work: the argument was that in reality it was the individual's perception of their own sickness that was leading them to believe themselves unfit for work. They believed that this incorrect perception could be easily be corrected, and on this basis they would be able to reduce the number of successful claims - from both state and private insurance providers.

However, it was James Purnell's leadership at the DWP which first propelled this new group of sick and disabled claimants on their journey towards activism. The premise of ESA had initially seemed reasonable - that some people were so sick and disabled they should be supported unconditionally, whilst others might be capable of some work under the right conditions and with the right support. But the means by which people were to be assessed, and the widespread introduction of sanctions to this vulnerable group, soon revealed its true motives, which, fundamentally, were aimed at reducing the number of claimants, based on the false idea that substantial numbers of claims were fraudulent. By 2007 the benefit scrounger rhetoric was increasing, and campaigns such as 'no ifs, no buts, benefit fraud is a crime' were becoming popular. But the MPs' expenses scandal in 2009, which included the revelation of claims by Purnell for large sums of money for his grocery

bills - which he claimed at a monthly rate higher than unemployment benefit levels
- encapsulated the hypocrisy of New Labour thinking for sick and disabled people,
and made Purnell a figure of fury as well as fear, thereby helping to sow the seeds of
more recent activism.[6]

There is a distinct irony in current disability rights politics: determined to create
his Big Society, David Cameron's only true step towards this has been to unify the
disabled community, who traditionally have been concerned with emphasising the
different needs and identities of each group. Unfortunately there are no political
allies on the horizon. Betrayed, abandoned and enraged by the welfare policies of
the New Labour years, disabled people already had our backs against the wall, and
the savagery of the cuts outlined in the comprehensive spending review are pushing
us over the edge. Respect for fellow members of our disabled community at one time
meant that Cameron had an easier ride on disability issues, because of his personal
experience as a son and father of a disabled person. But his willingness to use these
experiences as a campaign tactic has backfired, creating a deep anger and visceral
mistrust towards him personally.

The effects of deficit reduction on the disabled

Out of a total planned reduction in public spending of approximately £90 billion,
the cuts initially outlined by George Osborne that affect sick and disabled people are
estimated to total £9 billion: in other words, ten per cent of the overall cuts burden
will fall upon the most vulnerable in society.[7] These cuts are so wide ranging that it
is impossible to provide a truly comprehensive list, particularly as sick and disabled
people are more heavily reliant than most on NHS and local authority services; for
the purposes of this article only those cuts directly affecting employment prospects
will be considered.

Sick and disabled people feel that we are living in a horror story worthy of
Poe, as more and more of the vital supports we rely upon for daily life are either
removed or made significantly more difficult to access. Time and energy that is
already limited by health conditions will now have to be spent upon increasingly
fruitless applications for support, thus creating additional barriers to the possibility
of employment.[8] There has been no consideration of this conundrum in the
government's current plan to transfer a million people from sickness and disability

The benefits scandal

income replacement benefits into the totals for jobseeker allowance. If suitable accommodation, equipment and support were freely available, sick and disabled people would feel more confident about the potential of employment, but with that support being withdrawn from every direction, for many of us it feels as though we are in a pit, with the walls closing in upon us and no route of escape to be found. We are being simultaneously deprived of the support we need to be able to work and demonised for not working.

Accessible social housing is also woefully inadequate and poorly allocated, so that many disabled people are forced to rent homes which are not fully accessible in the more costly private sector (approximately 78,000 households in England that include a wheelchair user survive in premises that are not fully accessible).[9] The planned introduction of provision for an additional bedroom for a non-resident carer is a welcome step, but this extra funding will not be awarded automatically, and will be time limited in most cases to a maximum of thirteen weeks; while claimants under 35 will receive the 'shared room' rate, with exemptions only for those in receipt of middle or higher rate DLA. And the proposal to scrap DLA makes it impossible to fully assess the impact of these changes. Meanwhile the reduction of Local Housing Allowance (housing benefit), which was previously payable at the level of median average rents, but now will only be payable at the level of the bottom third, will force disabled people to rent cheaper properties that are more likely to be inaccessible. Contradictions in policy mean that DLA recipients are exempt from the caps on housing benefit, but not from the lowering of the levels of rent payable, which will have far wider effects. Suitable accessible accommodation removes many of the barriers to daily living faced by disabled people, making them more confident in considering employment, but it will be even harder to obtain once all these changes to entitlement take effect.

Mobility is another area that will be affected by cuts. The proposal to remove entitlement to the higher rate mobility component of Disability Living Allowance from state funded care home residents caused such outrage that the government have temporarily postponed the decision. But cuts to various council funded community transport schemes mean that disabled people are likely to face cost increases of more than 65 per cent, and for vastly restricted travel services.[10] Much of the current transport network is inaccessible to disabled people, so that reduced funding for alternatives will further restrict travel, and have an impact upon people's ability to travel to and from work.

The Coalition government also intend to scrap DLA altogether, and to replace it with Personal Independence Payment (PIP), which will involve reassessing all DLA recipients from 2013, even those with lifelong degenerative conditions - at vast cost, and with the aim of further reduction to entitlement, currently estimated at 20 per cent. There are many flaws in the proposed PIP, but for the purposes of this discussion the main impact will be felt in the removal of payments for the additional costs that dealing with disability requires, which will limit the ability of sick and disabled adults to remain in work, given that the funds they use to support these additional needs are to be withdrawn.

Social care is also affected - changes to its provision, people's entitlement and charges will be affected by a number of factors, including the scrapping of the Independent Living Fund, which matched funding from local authorities for those with the highest level of support needs. Furthermore, despite government insistence that cuts in funding to local authorities should not lead to any need to reduce social care provision, areas such as Birmingham are already planning to restrict support to those that meet a threshold of care that is higher than the four bands set out in the government's fair access to care services guidance; whilst most local authorities intend to increase charges.[11] Yet, without assistance in performing basic daily activities such as washing, dressing, shopping or eating, considering employment is impossible for many.

Access to Work is a government scheme that provides funding for disability-related equipment in order to assist working disabled people in carrying out their roles (for example it can pay for voice activated software or specialist chairs). It supported 37,000 disabled workers in 2009-10; worryingly but not surprisingly, the figure fell to 35,830 in 2010-11.[12] Now the Sayce Report, published in June 2011, is seeking to redefine what items it is 'reasonable' to expect an employer, rather than the government, to provide for disabled employees.[13] However, these items are frequently extremely expensive, which means that expecting employers to pay for them is likely to see a further reduction in opportunities for disabled people at work.[14] The proposed list of items that employers are now to be expected to pay for will make it significantly more expensive to hire a disabled employee. Reports of disabled employees being denied access to work support have already emerged, for example one application was refused because of a stipulation that if people are working in senior positions they should be funded by their employer regardless of their ability to bear the costs.[15]

The ESA labyrinth

When it was initially proposed, one of the ideas of the Employment Support Allowance was that disabled and sick people should be helped and supported to work if they wished to do so. This was a valid and popular idea. Many sick or disabled people would indeed love to work if there was work that they could do. But in its present form the ESA is failing: it simply presents the claimant with a series of dead ends, backed up by a whole raft of sanctions and means tests that negate any realistic chance of success. It takes little account of the limitations of individual conditions, or the barriers to work that someone with a fluctuating or mental health condition may face. The capability tests that are applied to claimants are simply unfit for purpose. Currently around 40 per cent of cases go to appeal, and of these 40 per cent succeed in overturning the original decision, a figure that rises to 70 per cent for those with representation.[16]

To qualify for ESA, an applicant must score fifteen points or more during a Work Capability Assessment (WCA). Anyone who scores less than 15 points will be found immediately 'fit for work' and moved onto Job Seekers Allowance (JSA). Leaving aside the limitations of the point system itself (which is dealt with below), there is an evident problem for those who score up to 14 points, and live with significant functional limitations, but whose score denies them the support and assistance of the Work Related Activity Group (WRAG). (The WRAG are those who are considered fit for work if support and preparation is provided. Only those receiving enough points to be allocated to the Support Group are not required to undertake work-related activity.) Those who fail to score 15 points must now compete with able-bodied applicants for work available through the Job Centre. If an applicant is then considered unfit for work by Jobcentre staff, they are passed backwards and forwards indefinitely, between JSA and unsuccessful ESA applications. These claimants are not tracked by the DWP, so no-one really knows how many go on to find work and how many simply fall through the cracks.

To compound this, the Work Capability Assessments and the descriptors they use are widely regarded as completely inadequate. They have been comprehensively criticised by a recent DWP report, as well as the professor who helped design the system, various charities and the Citizen's Advice Bureau.[17] They are simply not capable of assessing ability to work in any meaningful way. This leaves thousands receiving the wrong assessment, forced immediately into a workplace that they may not be ready for. Currently, 39 per cent of overall claimants are found immediately fit for work. Many of these people will have been away from the workplace for a considerable length of time, and some will have lifelong conditions.

Those placed into the WRAG (currently around 30 per cent of existing claims, and just 18 per cent of new claims) face many of the same problems. The descriptors used in the points system take no account of pain or symptoms or fatigue; they simply take a snapshot of what a person may or may not be able to do on the particular day of their assessment. Those with fluctuating conditions, which is particularly the case for those with mental health conditions or learning difficulties, are unlikely to be fairly assessed under the present system.[18]

With the proposed introduction of a one year time limit for those in the WRAG, almost all of the positives of ESA have been removed: after one year, whether or not their condition has improved, a claimant will now lose contributory ESA. Yet when it was designed, ESA was supposed to give sick and disabled people in the WRAG support for as long as it might take for them to enter work. The time limit removes any pretence at supporting the vulnerable, and turns ESA into a benefit that only supports conditions from which one might expect to recover within one year.

This means that if those with incurable or long-term chronic conditions are not placed in the Support Group category, thereby qualifying for unconditional long-term support, those with working partners will after one year find themselves totally dependent on them, and with no independent financial support. Currently just 7 per cent of new claimants are placed in the Support Group, meaning that thousands are faced with work sanctions that they cannot meet.

A clearly failing system breeds fear and suspicion within the disabled community, making them less likely to successfully engage with the scheme. At the same time the well publicised numbers of those suffering from its sanctions feed into the widespread assumption that those who are unwell or disabled are too lazy to work or just haven't tried hard enough. In our experience, this could not be further from the truth.[19] Removing security and support will simply exacerbate many conditions, creating further pressure on the NHS and local authorities. Most people who become

The benefits scandal

unable to work have tried many different ways of re-engaging with the workplace, but find employers unwilling to give them a chance, hours that are too long, or too rigid, or simply have to give up if their conditions worsen.

The rigidity of the current benefit system is incredibly daunting. With the proposed six-month qualifying period for DLA (it is currently three months), and a lengthy application process for ESA, claimants live in fear of giving up benefits to take a job in case they lose everything if they subsequently become unable to work again. A fairer system would offer a basic level of support to those with diagnosed conditions with a clear pathology, which could be tapered off as work is undertaken, yet readily available again if work becomes impossible or simply not financially sustainable.

Furthermore, if the system is to be rolled out to nearly 2 million people, relying on the assumption that they will be supported into work, then we should be very sure that the work programmes that have been charged with supporting claimants are operating successfully. But this is currently not the case. Pathways to Work, the programme which until very recently was responsible for assisting those on IB and ESA into work, has been found to have hardly any greater a success rate than claimants who are trying to find work on their own. Hundreds of millions of pounds have been paid out to private companies to help the sick and disabled into work, but, as Richard Disney et al explain:

> Preliminary evidence from the trial evaluations suggested that these programmes [i.e. Pathways] had a significant impact on the outflow from disability insurance [i.e. IB] in the first six months of the spell, but little effect thereafter, and that the effect was focused more on some work disability conditions (mostly physical) than others (mostly mental).[20]

In other words, those with more temporary conditions are 'helped' into work that they would have been very likely to find otherwise, whilst those with longer-term illnesses or disabilities are overwhelmingly let down by the system.

The truth is that pain, fatigue, nausea, dizziness, diarrhoea and many other symptoms are debilitating and disabling in their own right. We simply cannot wave a magic wand and expect people with serious, long-term conditions to be able to work in the way that an able bodied person usually can. Currently, 1 in 4 people of working age have some kind of illness or disability, and 60 per cent of them are already in work.[21]

With the rise in auto-immune conditions and long-term variable illnesses, and increased survival rates for many with congenital disabilities, the numbers of people living with long-term severe disability have risen, along with the numbers claiming DLA, whilst those claiming ESA alone have fallen.[22] People are living longer, but many are being kept alive with a host of complex and expensive medications and treatments that simply were not available three decades ago. Just as we face a crisis in elderly care and pension provision, we also face a crisis of increasing levels of people living with severe disability and long-term sickness - a trend seen throughout the wealthy world. Closing our eyes to these problems won't make them go away.

Alternative ways of contributing

People living with the most severe conditions present us with an opportunity to look in a new way at the very nature of 'work' and 'contribution'. People with long-term illnesses or disabilities need an entirely different set of solutions to those who are able-bodied. A system of fully flexible working hours would potentially allow the individual to dip in and out of work as and when they were able to. The hard and fast division between 'full-time' and 'part-time' is simply too limiting. However, a system could be designed whereby this flexible work could be underpinned by a contract allowing pro-rata payments, possibly with government working in partnership with employers. Such a scheme could only operate on the basis of reliability and security when someone attempts to leave benefits and enter the workplace. It would also need to be large enough to be truly viable on a national level. At the same time, we could do much more in today's technological age to enable those with long term illnesses or disabilities to work from home in pockets of time that suit their limitations.

Those who become too ill to continue their chosen careers may be able to re-train or study for new qualifications, allowing their employer to continue employing them in different roles. However, unless this kind of support is available at the point when an illness or disability becomes too debilitating, many will simply lose their jobs, and then they will find it many times more difficult to get another one when the particular crisis has passed, or re-education has been completed. But as I write, education for sick and disabled people is being reduced, not extended.[23]

A further option for many sick or disabled people would be to develop a hobby or small business idea into paid employment, which they would be more likely to have the confidence to do with a little support. Help to start and develop a small business, or even local business co-operatives, could remove much of the fear of failure that is inherent in starting any business, particularly when the entrepreneur is often unwell or unable to work.

Finally, government needs to engage with business, finding ways that those currently excluded from the workplace may again be included. They would do well to consider how the money already spent on welfare might be better targeted in the cases of those who wish to work but also need some time off or support in order to be able to do so. Transferring some of the welfare bill towards employers who are prepared or able to accept people with more variable limitations might remove some of the concerns that people have about fiscal responsibility. Some countries - for example Germany - mandate employers to hire a specific percentage of sick or disabled workers. Whether Britain adopts a similar scheme, or focuses on tax incentives and grants, we must start to take more note of the practicalities of employing someone with an illness or disability, and look at ways of supporting employers to do so.

It is, however, vitally important to remember that many people simply will not be able to work, and that sanctions and penalties will not create any miracle cures. But this is not to say that sick and disabled people cannot contribute in other ways. Many already volunteer or engage with their local communities, as and when they are able to. It may be unrealistic to expect those who are seriously unwell or severely disabled to fit into a traditional working model, but it is unhelpful to ignore the great contribution they can and already do make to society.

Any system that truly aims to reward responsibility, or claims to be based on fairness, must adopt a holistic approach to the idea of contribution. Those that find themselves unable to be reliably financially productive may yet be productive in many other ways. This contribution should not be ignored or dismissed, but should be part of the overall assessment of what a person can or cannot do. Politicians are currently very keen on the ideas of contribution and responsibility, but if that is

Soundings

simply taken to mean an ability to bring in a financially viable wage, it will inevitably exclude a whole sector of society with different needs and abilities.

Kaliya Franklin is a disability rights campaigner, writer and blogger (www.benefitscroungingscum.blogspot.com). She is a co-founder of the non-partisan group The Broken of Britain (www.thebrokenofbritain.blogspot.com), who campaign against the punitive measures in the Welfare Reform Bill and for disability rights. **Sue Marsh** suffers from severe crohn's disease and campaigns to raise awareness of fluctuating conditions, and the effect that welfare reform has on sick and disabled people in the UK. She writes the blog, Diary of a Benefit Scrounger (diaryofabenefitscrounger.blogspot.com/), and is political strategist for the Broken of Britain. She also writes for *The Guardian* and prominent left-wing blogs such as Left Foot Forward, Labour List and Liberal Conspiracy.

Notes

1. See for example www.dailymail.co.uk/news/article-1353111/Disability-benefits-Half-claimants-asked-prove-eligibility.html.

2. For recent government statistics on DLA claimants see http://statistics.dwp.gov.uk/asd/asd1/adhoc_analysis/2011/DLA_Growth_in_Caseload_FINAL.pdf.

3. See BBC news reports: http://news.bbc.co.uk/1/hi/uk/politics/33556.stm; http://news.bbc.co.uk/1/hi/uk/41746.stm.

4. For more on the myth that there are one million people on benefits who are really fit for work, see Steve Griffiths, 'The misuse of evidence in incapacity benefit reform', *Soundings* 47: www.lwbooks.co.uk/journals/soundings/articles/s47griffiths.pdf

5. For more on the biopsychosocial model, see Jonathan Rutherford, 'New Labour, the market state, and the end of welfare':

www.lwbooks.co.uk/journals/articles/rutherford07.html.

6. 'Minister puts food bill on expenses', *Sunday Express*, 12.4.09.

7. See www.scope.org.uk/news/disabled-people-hit-by-welfare-cuts.

The benefits scandal

8. See for example my own story - Kaliya Franklin, 'Being turned down for an electric wheelchair has left me dejected', *Guardian*, 4.8.11: www.guardian.co.uk/society/joepublic/2011/aug/04/denied-electric-wheelchair-nhs-criteria.

9. See www.disabledgo.com/blog/2010/08/solutions-to-housing-shortage-are-not-complicated/.

10. For an example of local cuts to community transport see www.sunderlandecho.com/news/local/end_of_the_line_for_shoppers_bus_1_2849126.

11. See www.communitycare.co.uk/Articles/2010/12/02/115939/storm-of-protest-greets-birminghams-super-critical-threshold.htm; and www.communitycare.co.uk/Articles/2010/07/01/114824/care-charges-set-to-soar-for-users-in-warwickshire.htm.

12. www.candocango.com/government-ignores-alarm-bells-as-access-to-work-figures-slump/.

13. www.dwp.gov.uk/docs/sayce-report.pdf.

14. For examples of exclusions see www.abilitymagazine.org.uk/Articles/Article-108-3.aspx.

15. www.candocango.com/fury-as-government-denies-disabled-leader-access-to-work/.

16. http://www.legislation.gov.uk/uksi/2011/228/pdfs/uksi_20110228_en.pdf

17. See www.publications.parliament.uk/pa/cm201012/cmselect/cmworpen/1015/101505.htm; www.guardian.co.uk/commentisfree/2010/jul/06/osborne-haste-undermine-incapacity-benefit-reform; www.guardian.co.uk/politics/2011/mar/09/welfare-bill-cancer-patients; www.citizensadvice.org.uk/press_20100323.

18. See Malcolm Harrington, *An independent review of the work capability assessment*, HMSO 2010, www.dwp.gov.uk/docs/wca-review-2010.pdf.

19. http://diaryofabenefitscrounger.blogspot.com/2011/05/welfare-for-people-by-people.html.

20. R. Disney et al, 'The baby-boomers at fifty…', in P. Gregg and J. Wadsworth (eds) *The Labour market in winter: the state of working Britain*, Oxford 2011, p67.

21. 'Baby-boomers at fifty', see note 20.

22. See Declan Gaffney in this issue.

24. www.disabledgo.com/blog/2011/08/government-could-face-new-high-court-challenge-over-cuts/

'Dependency' and disability: how to misread the evidence on social security

Declan Gaffney

Contemporary narratives on 'welfare dependency' turn on airbrushing long-term disability out of the evidence.

———

Both left and right have a tendency to treat out-of-work benefit receipt as a symptom of broad societal malaise - whether this is seen in terms of the failures of capitalism, or of moral decline, or (increasingly, on both sides) of both. But neither of these perspectives is appropriate for the purposes of discussing a system that mainly deals with situations which would need to be addressed by any functioning welfare state, under any plausible economic circumstances or social values: i.e., assistance in periods of temporary unemployment or sickness, and for longer periods of severe and long-term disabling conditions and caring responsibilities.

The sort of grandstanding references to 'six million people on welfare' that dominate political debate in this area involve airbrushing out of the picture these routine functions of the benefits system, in favour of shadowy social archetypes: families where 'no one has worked for generations', communities where 'no one works around here', 'the underclass'.[1] The conflation of social security and social

'Dependency' and disability

dysfunction is one of the dominant tropes of current debate on welfare on all sides. Will Hutton, on the centre left, could declare last year that 'the welfare state was not set up to support vast families or single mothers in intergenerational welfare dependency' - the question of whether it was to any significant extent doing anything of the kind was not even posed.[2]

It is well known that social security systems can have intended and unintended effects that go well beyond their function of managing social risks. However, the extent to which any system does have negative effects is essentially an empirical issue rather than a matter for intuition; but the sort of accusations that have been levelled against the UK system by commentators on left and right have rarely been supported with relevant, up-to-date data on who claims out-of-work benefits, why, and, crucially, for how long. Indeed most assertions on 'welfare dependency' turn on an implicit and quite erroneous assumption that benefit claims are overwhelmingly long-term in nature.

This article looks at the area of the benefits system that is most relevant to discussions that present long-term benefit receipt as a symptom or a cause of societal problems - i.e. those in receipt of incapacity and disability benefits, which now account for some 81 per cent of all long-term out-of-work claims (claims running for five years or over). To understand the underlying trends within this group we begin with the history of economic inactivity and benefit receipt from the early 1980s to the mid-1990s, since this history continues to influence contemporary anxieties about social security.[3] We then look at the period from 1997 to the present, and in particular at contrasting developments in the 'incapacity' and 'disability' caseloads. We show that the idea that Labour failed to reduce the Incapacity Benefit (IB) caseload - a dominant theme in the party's post-election autopsy - is largely a myth, and is based on misconceptions about the geography, age and gender patterns of benefit receipt. In fact IB receipt fell substantially during this period, and fell most for age groups and areas with the highest levels of receipt. On the other hand disability benefit receipt rose during this period (albeit not as much as incapacity benefit receipt fell), partly because of demographic factors, but also because of increases in claims associated with mental health and learning difficulties. On the other hand there was no rise in disability benefit claims associated with physical conditions.

The key point here is that long-term out of work benefit receipt is increasingly dominated by people living with more severe disabling conditions, and by people caring for the disabled. And neither the flaws of contemporary capitalism nor changes in social values have much of a role in explaining these trends or indicating promising policy directions.

'Incapacity and disability' benefits in the UK fall into two groups. The first group consists of income replacement benefits, whether contributions-based or income-based: Incapacity Benefit (IB), or, for those who do not meet the contributions conditions, income support for reason of sickness or disability. For new claimants, these benefits have been replaced since October 2008 with Employment Support Allowance (ESA), and existing IB claimants are currently being transferred to the new benefit. In most statistical discussion, those in receipt of any income replacement benefit for reasons of sickness or disability are classed together as 'IB/ESA' claimants. We depart from this practice to make a distinction within the IB/ESA caseload, based on whether or not someone is in receipt of Disability Living Allowance.[4]

Disability Living Allowance (hereafter DLA), introduced in 1992, is a non-means tested benefit for people with disabilities which lead to specific mobility and care requirements. Eligibility conditions and administration are completely separate from those for the income replacement benefits (although some DLA entitlements affect entitlements to these and other benefits). It is paid at a variety of rates depending on the nature of the claimant's impairments, and a large proportion of awards are 'indefinite', i.e. claimants' conditions are not expected to improve over time. DLA is *not* an out-of-work benefit, and about a fifth of working age DLA recipients are not receiving an income replacement benefit.

This article focuses on the differences in trends between those receiving IB/ESA and those who receive DLA, most of whom also receive IB/ESA, in order to give a rounded picture of trends in incapacity and disability benefit receipt.[5]

Thirty years of incapacity and disability benefits

The historical labour market data of the 1980s and early 1990s documents a period of labour market trauma. At the time attention was largely focused on the return of unemployment at levels that had not seen for generations, but for our purposes there is particular significance in the accompanying major build-up of economic

'Dependency' and disability

inactivity (i.e. those neither working nor looking for work) among people of working age, which was to prove one of the most persistent legacies of the Thatcher era. The scale and rapidity of the changes can be illustrated by the fact that activity for men in the 55-59 age band fell from 91 per cent in 1980 to 80 per cent by 1987, and to 74 per cent by 1994. These changes did not contribute to the unemployment figures, as these former workers were not actively seeking work: many either took early retirement or were diverted on to incapacity and disability benefits. By 1995, of the 424,000 men aged 55-59 in receipt of benefits, some 71 per cent were receiving a sickness or disability benefit.[6]

The experience of rapid falls in economic activity for older men was international, affecting most western economies in the 1980s. While the scale and timing varied from country to country, common factors included the felt need on the part of employers to shed less 'productive' workers in the face of increased international competition, and a tendency towards labour rationing on the part of governments committed to employment-constraining deflationary policies - if the economy could no longer provide full employment, better if the jobs went to those with young families to support.[7]

This logic did not always extend to female parents. The UK saw rapid increases in employment for women in couples during the 1980s, but for the growing number of female lone parents the experience was the opposite, with employment falling from 63 per cent in 1980 to 44 per cent by 1995: again, this represented a growth in inactivity rather than unemployment, and, as with older men, the benefit system played a role in diverting claimants into inactivity, as lone parents were placed on income support rather than unemployment-related benefits.[8]

By the late 1990s benefits caseloads were dominated by economic inactivity rather than unemployment, and of these incapacity benefit (2.6 million) and income support for lone parents (995,000) were the most important elements.[9] There were also major disparities in IB receipt between areas, reflecting the geographical pattern of deindustrialisation and the collapse of mining, and substantial gender differences, especially among older claimants. Thus in Wales and the North East, IB claims for men aged 55-59 were equivalent to some 29 per cent of the population by 1999, compared to a national average for men in this age band of 19 per cent and for women of 15 per cent. More than a million IB claims had been running for five years or more. This was, broadly, the situation that

Soundings

Labour inherited in 1997.

So far we have followed the standard story on the rise in incapacity benefit receipt: however it is clear that there was more going on during this period than government exploitation of the benefits system to manage deindustrialisation and slack labour demand. It has long been recognised in the academic literature that the prevalence of disability, as measured by survey data, did in fact increase from the 1970s to the mid-1990s. Richard Berthoud found that the percentage of the population reporting a long-standing limiting illness rose from 14 per cent in 1975 to 18 per cent in 1995.[10] However, this rise in self-reported disability has often been interpreted, largely without evidence, as reflecting a greater willingness of people to define themselves as disabled, rather than any substantial change in the prevalence of disability within population: there was for a long time an informational vacuum due to lack of statistical evidence on the severity of disability among the growing self-reported disabled population. It was not until Berthoud's 2011 paper that evidence on disability trends at different levels of severity was brought into play; and this indicated that disability prevalence had risen at *all* levels of severity, and at a somewhat greater rate for the most severely impaired.

It now looks as if the rise in incapacity and disability benefit receipt up to the mid-1990s was underpinned by three broad processes, each with differing timings and tempos: there was a gradual rise in disability prevalence between the late 1970s and the mid 1990s; there was at the same time a steady deterioration of the employment chances of disabled people at all levels of severity; and there was a pronounced geographical variation in IB receipt, caused by the concentration in certain areas of the accumulated impacts of weak labour demand and deindustrialisation.[11] While it is likely that government policy played a role in making a worsening situation even worse, by diverting unemployed workers on to incapacity and disability benefits, there were clearly other factors at work in driving benefit caseloads to the high levels they had reached by the mid-1990s, and in maintaining these levels during Labour's period in office. However, by 1997 the assumption that the rise in incapacity and disability benefit receipt was entirely due to 'labour market' factors or 'welfare dependency' was thoroughly engrained. In 1999, Tony Blair roundly declared the IB was 'not a benefit which compensates those who have had to give up work because of long-term illness or sickness - it's an alternative to long-term unemployment or early retirement. That's why it must

'Dependency' and disability

be reformed'.[12]

From 1997 to 2002, Labour oversaw what was arguably the most radical period of social security reform since the foundation of the welfare state, with the introduction of the minimum wage, an unprecedented expansion of in-work financial support, important steps towards integration of the tax and benefit system, the establishment of Sure Start (later, Children's Centres), the introduction of a range of 'New Deals' for different categories of benefit claimant and the adoption of the target of eliminating child poverty by 2020. Contrary to what seems to be widely believed, Labour also reformed Incapacity Benefit in 1999, tightening contributions conditions.

The chart below summarises developments for the two main 'inactive' groups inherited from the previous administrations over Labour's period in office. The contrast between lone parents and IB claimants could hardly be more striking - or, as we shall see later, more deceptive. On the face of it, lone parent benefit receipt reduced dramatically, while the IB caseload remained largely unchanged. This stability was to become the major premise of those arguing the need for 'radical' reform of IB, which became something of a totemic issue for Blair towards the end of his period as prime minister.

There is, it must be said, something rather implausible about this picture. Under Labour, unemployment fell to its lowest level for a generation, and the

Chart 1 Receipt of main out-of-work benefits 1997-2011 (1997=1)

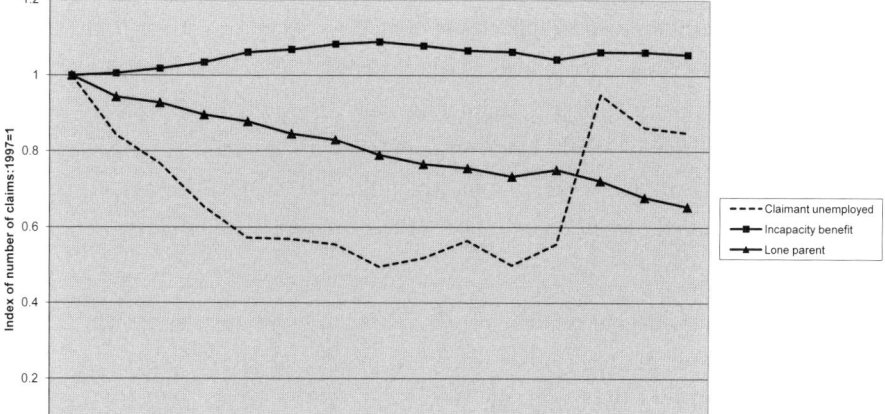

combination of the minimum wage and tax credits should have improved the gains from working for the lower-skilled workers who dominated the IB caseload. That these changes should have had no effect whatsoever on IB receipt therefore strains credulity. And indeed, when we look at receipt by age, gender and geography, it becomes clear that IB receipt did fall, and it fell most where rates had been highest: in former industrial and mining areas, among older workers, and among men. A simple analysis of the caseload between 1999 and 2010 shows that falls in rates of receipt among men over this period equated to some 19 per cent of the 1999 caseload, but that this was offset by the effects of population ageing; these increased the total by the equivalent of 10 per cent, resulting in a net fall of only 9 per cent. Reductions in rates of receipt were concentrated in the North of England, Wales and Scotland, where rates had risen most during the 1980s and 1990s. Among women, whose rates of receipt were generally lower, there was a slight rise in overall receipt, and this was entirely explained by ageing. Unpicking these opposing influences shows that the immobility of the IB caseload was something of a myth. This becomes even more apparent when we look at compositional changes in the caseload in the next section.

An alternative perspective on benefit receipt

So far we have talked of 'incapacity and disability' benefits, ignoring the heterogeneity of situations that the benefits system needs to support. Many claimants experience relatively short-term episodes of work-limiting illness: others have severe conditions which will last for the rest of their lives; while yet others are in situations between the extremes of severity and duration. There is no single, objective methodology for partitioning the claimant population on criteria of severity and duration of conditions. However, we can exploit the fact that the UK has a separate and non-means tested benefit specifically for the more severely disabled to explore the composition of benefit caseloads.

To explain: many benefit claimants are in receipt of more than one benefit, and in order to avoid double counting of claimants, official data on benefit receipt from the Department of Work and Pensions and the Office for National Statistics conventionally groups claims for different combinations of benefits into statistical groups (jobseekers, lone parents, disabled, etc) according to a hierarchy in which

'Dependency' and disability

certain benefits and reasons for claiming take precedence over others in deciding which group a claimant will be allocated to. Importantly for our purposes, a DLA recipient who is in receipt of IB/ESA will be allocated to the 'ESA and incapacity benefits' group rather than to the 'disabled' group. The official 'disabled' statistical group includes only the (growing) minority of DLA recipients who are not receiving an income replacement benefit.

In this section we use an alternative grouping, in which DLA receipt takes precedence over IB/ESA receipt in allocating recipients to groups. In other words, we are more interested here in whether people are receiving DLA - an indicator of the severity of their impairment - than in whether or not they are receiving an income replacement benefit. The totals for incapacity and disability benefits (table 2, right hand column) confirm that our alternative grouping uses the same underlying data as the DWP groups and does not lead to double counting or undercounting of claimants.

This is not, it should be stressed, an attempt to distinguish 'disabled' from 'non-disabled' benefit recipients. In particular, it is not the case that DLA receipt marks out a group which is unable to work, because many DLA recipients are working, while not all work-limiting conditions will necessarily lead to DLA eligibility. Evidence on claim durations suggests that a substantial minority of IB recipients who are not receiving DLA have long-term conditions, but nevertheless IB recipients who are also receiving DLA are far more likely to be long-term claimants.

It is worth dwelling on this point, given that the pattern of claim duration for IB recipients is the subject of considerable confusion. Statements to the effect that the great majority of IB claims are long-term in duration are common, and are often used to suggest that IB has a quasi-magical power to induce long-term benefit dependency. In fact, the arithmetic of stocks and flows means that at any point in time, long-term claims (i.e. longer than five years) form a clear majority of the IB caseload. In the same way, a census of in-patients in a hospital ward would show a preponderance of older patients with longer lengths of stay. However, if we wanted to calculate the average length of stay for all in-patient admissions, we would not count patients at a single point in time, as this would give us an upwardly biased estimate: we would look at all admissions over an extended period. The same applies to benefit caseloads.

This point is illustrated in Table 1 below, using data from 2003-2008. The point-in-time estimate for 2008 shows that a majority (61 per cent) of IB claims in

Table 1 Distribution of incapacity benefit claims by claim duration (approximate)[14]

		<1 year	<2 years	<5 years	5 years +
All IB claims	2008	13.4	21.5	38.8	61.2
All IB claims	2003-2008	37.8	47.8	62.8	37.2
		<1 year	<2 years	<5 years	5 years +
All IB claims excluding DLA combinations	2008	23.7	35.3	56.2	43.8
All IB claims excluding DLA combinations	2003-2008	50.8	62.4	77.3	22.7
		<1 year	<2 years	<5 years	5 years +
IB/DLA combinations	2008	4.1	4.9	14.0	76.9
IB/DLA combinations	2003-2008	7.7	6.3	15.1	70.9

Source: DWP benefit flows tabulation tool (flows); WPLS (stock).[14]

payment had run for five years or more. Over five years, however, this percentage is 37 per cent. When we exclude claims which include DLA, the point-in-time share of long term cases falls to 44 per cent, while the five-year estimate is 23 per cent. This is a substantial minority of non-DLA IB claims, but it is clear that long-term claims for this group were the exception, not the rule, over this period. Half of claims ended within a year and 62 per cent within two years. For claims which include DLA, however, 71 per cent lasted five years or more.

This striking difference in the pattern of claim durations shows how important it is to take account of DLA in looking at trends in IB receipt. It is well known that the amount of time people spend on IB was a more important driver of growth in caseload numbers than any changes in the number of people coming on to IB. An increase in the share of DLA-entitled recipients of IB, other things being equal, implies an increase in the share of long-term claims, with a greater impact on overall caseload numbers over the longer term than an equivalent increase for other types of claimant, who are much more likely to leave the benefit within a relatively short period. Figures on long-term benefit receipt in particular should be contextualised in terms of DLA, to avoid the risk of misleading inferences - for example, that IB/ESA taken on its own tends to encourage long-term benefit receipt.[13]

Comparison with the DWP groups shows the point of our regrouping of the data (Table 2). Our 'disability' group based on DLA receipt is more than four times the size of the DWP 'disability' group in 2010, while our 'ESA/IB' group, which excludes DLA claimants, is just half the size of the DWP group. In 2010, our 'disability' group is considerably larger than our 'ESA/IB' group, while the DWP 'IB/ESA' statistical group is some six times the size of the corresponding disabled group. The alternative grouping brings out what is surely one of the more important aspects of contemporary benefit receipt: a clear majority of all incapacity and disability benefit recipients have conditions severe enough to entitle them to DLA - something which

'Dependency' and disability

Table 2 DWP and alternative groupings of incapacity and disability benefit claims

		Year	ESA and Incapacity Benefits	Disability	Total
DWP statistical groups		2002	2,765,220	256,230	3,021,450
Alternative grouping*		2002	1,601,280	1,420,190	3,021,470
DWP statistical groups		2010	2,576,240	398,880	2,975,120
Alternative grouping*		2010	1,279,450	1,695,700	2,975,150
DWP statistical groups	numerical change 2002-2010		-188,980	142,650	-46,330
Alternative grouping*	numerical change 2002-2010		-321,830	275,510	-46,320
DWP statistical groups	% change 2002-2010		-6.8	55.7	-1.5
Alternative grouping*	% change 2002-2010		-20.1	19.4	-1.5

Decomposition of change by age band 2002-2010

		ESA and Incapacity Benefits	Disability	Total
Alternative grouping	% change due to demography	5.2	6.6	11.8
	% change due to rate of receipt	-25.3	12.8	-12.5
	% change	-20.1	19.4	-0.7

** In the 'alternative grouping', 'disability' includes all receiving DLA, while ESA and IB excludes those in receipt of DLA; for the DWP, the ESA and IB group also includes those who also receive DLA, while its 'disability' group includes people in receipt solely of DLA.

Source: Work and Pensions Longitudinal Study

is obscured by the precedence given to IB/ESA receipt in the DWP's grouping.

The alternative grouping also offers a different perspective on changes in benefit receipt over time. Both groupings show numerical falls in the 'ESA/IB' group and rises in the 'disabled' group between 2002 and 2010, but the scale of these changes is almost doubled in the alternative grouping.

The long-term development of the incapacity and disability caseload using our alternative grouping is shown in chart 2, which combines data from two DWP datasets covering different timeframes (as can be seen from the overlap between the two from 2002 to 2007, they give broadly consistent results). Disability benefit claims have risen more or less continuously since the introduction of DLA, and have exceeded IB-only claims since 2004. Note that these figures include people who are only receiving DLA, many of whom will be working: this group, while it forms a minority of DLA claims, has in fact shown by far the strongest growth since 2002. IB/ESA-only claims have been falling since 2002, but this then levelled out with the onset of recession. Some of these changes of course reflect transfers between the two groups, but in the absence of published longitudinal data tracking individual claimants over time, we are unable to quantify this.

We can however separate out the demographic component of these changes, as we did earlier for IB/ESA totals. In fact the 20.1 per cent fall in the IB/ESA-only caseload is composed of a 25 per cent reduction due to falling rates of receipt by age and gender, offset by a 5 per cent increase due to population changes. (For men the reduction by rates of receipt is some 31 per cent of the 2002 caseload, offset by a 7 per cent increase due to population. For women demographic change raised the caseload by 3 per cent while reduced receipt lowered it by 18 per cent.)

Soundings

Chart 2 Incapacity and disability benefit receipt 1995-2010

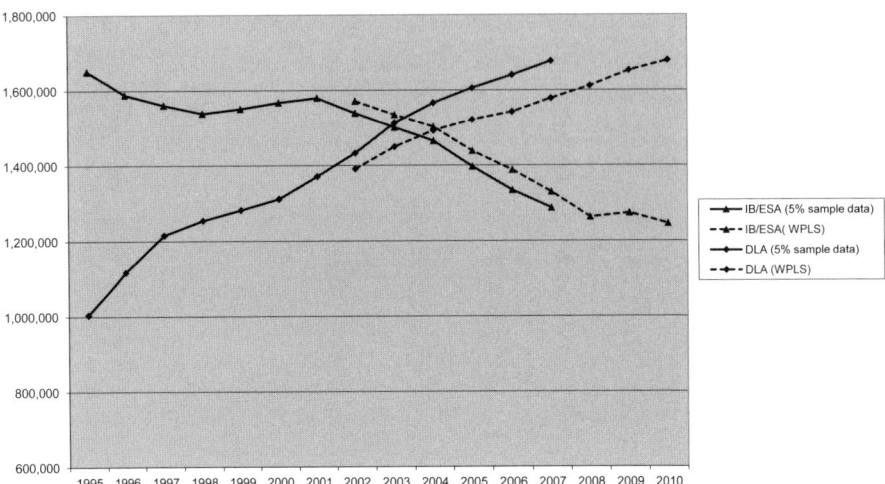

Thus the IB/ESA grouping as a whole, which is on average less severely impaired than the group in receipt of DLA, has seen a quite dramatic numerical reduction since 2002, especially among men, but this has been partially offset by demographic change. This contrasts with the upward trend for the 'disabled group', where demographic change explains only about a third of the increase. However, among those who are in receipt of both DLA and IB/ESA, demographic change has increased numbers of recipients by 6.5 per cent, compared to 5 per cent due to rising rates of receipt. In other words, demography alone explains more than half the increase in out-of-work DLA claims.

How should these contrasting trends be interpreted? Just over half the fall in IB/ESA-only receipt among men is accounted for by those aged 55-64: the retirement or death of those workers who shouldered the burden of the massive employment dislocations of earlier decades may be an important part of the overall change, but it is still only a part. Strong labour market performance up to the recession, coupled with policy changes (tax credits, minimum wage), are likely to be the main factors: the expected effect would be that those with less severe conditions would return to employment more quickly in tighter labour markets, gradually bringing down caseload numbers.[15] For women, the fall in caseload is more evenly spread over the age range, suggesting that changes affecting specific cohorts are less important than

'Dependency' and disability

among men. Labour's third term reforms are not central to these changes, as most of the fall took place before 2008.

As we have seen, more than half the rise in out-of-work DLA receipt is explained simply by demographic change: for those receiving DLA alone this explains only about 14 per cent. The extent to which we should see the remainder of the increase in DLA as an indication of a wider prevalence of disability - as an effect of the maturing of the DLA system (i.e. people being more likely to claim) or as a side effect of policies of deinstitutionalisation - remains an open question. Two things are clear, however. The rises in DLA receipt over this period are not due to increased flows of claimants on to the benefit (these have fallen), but to the gradual build-up of claims of long duration.[16] And once we adjust for demographic change, there has been no increase in DLA receipt associated with physical conditions: the diagnostic groups which account for the increase are learning difficulties and mental health.[17] Any explanation of the rise in DLA is therefore likely to turn on changes in the way people with mental health problems and learning difficulties are supported, rather than on some general factor such as 'welfare dependency' or 'hidden unemployment'.

Conclusion

Bringing demographic change and severity of impairment into the picture in this way raises obvious questions about the aggressive benefit caseload reduction aims adopted by both the current and previous governments ('a million off IB'). If the IB/ESA-only group has already fallen by a quarter (controlling for demography), and by nearly a third among men, one has to ask how much further this part of the caseload can be expected to be reduced if the system is to continue to provide social protection for those experiencing short and medium term incapacity for work. Changes to work incentives through tried and tested welfare reform interventions are likely to yield diminishing returns given the current composition of the caseload, which reflects in part the success of previous social security reform. Rather, the focus needs to be on a realistic assessment of employment chances for people with more severe conditions, and long-term effort to improve these chances, involving all relevant policy instruments. The current moralising and grievance-laden discourse of welfare is a formidable barrier to any such positive developments.

This article has tried to give a sense of the out-of-work benefit system we have as opposed to the largely symbolic construction which dominates current debate. This is a system which is primarily engaged in dealing with spells of work-limiting illness and unemployment, and with longer term periods of severe disability and caring responsibilities. While it is far from perfect, this system is unrecognisable as the 'road to dependency' of left and right welfare reform rhetoric; and, for the time being at least, it is in much better condition than it was in the aftermath of the deindustrialisation waves of the 1980s and early 1990s.

Notes

1. For a rigorous account exposing the lack of realism in claims that there are significant numbers of 'intergenerationally workless' families see L. Macmillan, 'Measuring the intergenerational correlation of worklessness', *CMPO Bulletin*, University of Bristol, September 2011; see also D. Gaffney, 'The myth of the intergenerational workless household', *Left Foot Forward*, 21.9.10: www.leftfootforward.org/2010/09/the-myth-of-the-intergenerational-workless-household/.

2. www.guardian.co.uk/commentisfree/2010/oct/10/fair-society-cameron-osborne.

3. We follow Ruth Lister in eschewing the term 'welfare', and for the same reasons. See her 'Our social security system must guarantee real welfare' *Guardian*, Comment is Free, 28.8.11: www.guardian.co.uk/commentisfree/2011/aug/28/robin-hood-poor-welfare.

4. Severe Disablement Allowance, an income replacement benefit for disabled people, was closed to new claimants in 2000. Our figures for both 'sickness' and 'disability' benefits include SDA claims. SDA claims are allocated to the 'disabled' group when combined with DLA.

5. Consistent data on DLA is generally only available from 2002 on, although we have devised a broadly consistent time series back to 1995. Much of the analysis therefore focuses on the period 2002-2010, which by coincidence saw major changes in incapacity and disability benefit caseloads.

'Dependency' and disability

6. DWP benefits 5 per cent sample data.

7. See European Commission, *Study of compilation of disability statistical data from the administrative registers of member states*, 2007, esp. p.17, p.25; see also I. Mares, 'Firms and the welfare state: when, why and how does social policy matter to employers?', in Hall and Soskice (eds.), *Varieties of capitalism*, Oxford 2001; and T. Iversen, *Capitalism, democracy and welfare*, Cambridge 2005.

8. Data on lone parent employment from R. Blundell, A. Bozio and G. Laroque, *Extensive and intensive margins of labour supply: working hours in the US, UK and France*, Institute for Fiscal Studies Working Paper, 01.11; male economic activity figures from International Labour Organisation, *Economically Active Population Estimates and Projections* (EAPEP) dataset.

9. Data for third quarter 1999 from Work and Pensions Longitudinal Study.

10. R. Berthoud, *The employment rates of disabled people*, DWP Research report No 298, 2006.

11. I am grateful to Ben Baumberg for advice on interpreting disability trends. Responsibility for the interpretation offered here rests with the author of course.

12. S. Griffiths, 'The misuse of evidence in incapacity benefit reform', in *Soundings* 47: www.lwbooks.co.uk/journals/soundings/articles/s47griffiths.pdf.

13. The hypothesised causal process here runs from underlying conditions to work-limiting impairment to long-term non-employment and therefore long-term IB receipt combined with DLA. In the alternative hypothesis, put forward by Beatty, Fothergill and Platts-Fowler (*DLA claimants: a new assessment*, DWP Research report no. 585, 2009) the process runs from long-term IB receipt to eventual DLA claims 'as further source of financial support': in other words, whatever drives IB-only receipt (primarily labour market factors, on this account) also drives IB/DLA receipt; and DLA is essentially an 'adjunct' to IB. Given the quite different eligibility conditions for DLA compared to IB, and the evidence on the differences between the IB/ESA-only and DLA caseloads, we think that much stronger evidence than has been offered thus far would be needed to displace the naive reading that care and mobility needs are the dominant explanatory factors for DLA receipt.

14. 'Claims' are calculated as the sum of off-flows over the period by duration

and benefit combination at off-flow, and the stock of claims (by duration and combination) at the end of the period. Percentages should be taken as illustrative only. To avoid spurious precision, rather than summing quarterly flows over the entire period we have simply multiplied the 2007-8 flows by five. Note that the benefit combinations are recorded at the point of off-flow or the end of the period: claimants will not necessarily have been on these particular combinations throughout the claim duration. Because these figures relate to the period 2003-2008, they are not affected by Labour's third term reforms to Incapacity Benefit. Flows data for DLA-only claims (the remainder of our 'disability' group absent from these figures) are not published.

15. For a similar interpretation of the overall fall in IB/ESA see D. McVicar, 'Local level incapacity benefit rolls in Britain: correlates and convergences', Queen's University School of Management, working paper, December 2009.

16. See D. Gaffney, 'The "inexplicable" rise of Disability Allowance explained', *Left Foot Forward*, 14.2.11: www.leftfootforward.org/2011/02/rise-in-disability-living-allowance-explained/.

17. See D. Gaffney, 'Clause 52 of the Welfare Reform Bill' (September 2011): http://lartsocial.org/pdf/Clause52oftheWelfareReformBill.pdf.

Cuts are a feminist issue

Feminist fightback collective

The government's cutbacks in social provision are privatising work that is crucial to the sustenance of life.

———

Since the Coalition government was 'elected' in the United Kingdom in May 2010, we have opened our newspapers each day to litanies of cuts to services - in health care; domestic violence services; universal child benefit; disability benefit; lone parent benefit; pensions; carer's allowance; housing benefit; education; free school meals; and early-years provision, to name only some. Such services constitute the means by which a people are kept healthy, fed, clothed, housed, educated and made into productive workers able to support the nation's economy. And the destruction of such public and common goods is not unique to the United Kingdom; over the last thirty years, despite their being essential to human life, neoliberal restructuring across the world has privatised, eroded and demolished our shared resources, and ushered in a 'crisis of social reproduction'.[1]

The term social reproduction encompasses all the means by which society reproduces its families, citizens and workers. It includes all the labour that is necessary for a society to reproduce itself: the biological production of people and workers, and all the social practices that sustain the population - bearing children, raising children, performing emotional work, providing clothing and food, and cooking and cleaning. As a concept social reproduction has been key to feminist social theory, because it challenges the usual distinctions that are made between productive and reproductive labour, or between the labour market and the home.

Soundings

Labour in this sphere is often devalued and privatised, and is typically performed by women in their 'double day' or 'second shift', alongside paid wage labour. But reproductive labour of this kind is just as central to capitalist accumulation as are other forms of labour, which means that struggles over its structure and distribution are fundamental to any understanding of issues of power and the relationships between labour and capital, as well as the potential for their transformation.

The austerity measures of the Coalition government will affect every facet of human life and relations; they are attempting to undermine the welfare state and to create a profoundly unequal society, and this will hit women particularly hard, as well as other marginalised and vulnerable groups. Such a disproportionate impact is not an unintended or unforeseen effect of the cuts. Rather, it is endemic to this government's drive to destroy the welfare state, and in particular to restructure existing forms of social reproduction. Exploring the focus, distribution and likely effects of this austerity programme through the lens of social reproduction allows us to better understand not only the uneven impacts it will have on different sectors of society, but also the ways in which it supports the production and accumulation of wealth, and its concentration into the hands of the few. And it may also point to sites of resistance and transformation.

As an anti-capitalist feminist collective based in East London, we have been organising around some of the immediate manifestations of such cuts - in the National Health Service and public services more broadly, and in their effects on nursery provision in the London boroughs of Hackney and Tower Hamlets in particular. Despite our practical emphasis on the local situation, we believe that our struggle to defend local provision can only be understood in a wider context: that of a crisis in care. In writing this article, our aim is not to simply make an inventory of the effects of the cuts, but to think about the wider assault on social reproduction that they represent, and to try to find some pathways in contesting this. We use 'the home' as a lens for understanding the constellation of social, economic and political processes at work in this programme of austerity - and the faultlines that may emerge to open a space for challenging them.

First we look at the specific nature of the current round of austerity and adjustment in the UK, arguing that - much like other instances of neoliberal structural adjustment - it has the effect of privatising survival and social reproduction, with the burden of labour falling on women. We focus on this not

Cuts are a feminist issue

because we think this is the only feminist issue, or is only an issue for feminists, but because we see it as a productive way into thinking about how to build a movement that can mount a much broader challenge to the austerity drive. We outline the multiple insidious effects of this culture and economics of austerity on women themselves, and on divisions of labour, communities and social justice. We end by seeking to highlight many of the contradictions of the cuts, which we suggest might become the 'cracks' out of which can emerge a movement that fights for an alternative way of organising our lives, outlining what a 'feminist' movement against the cuts might look like.

The Big Society: coming soon to a home near you

The home occupies a pivotal site in the flows and processes of austerity measures. State retrenchment and privatisation force the labour of social reproduction back into the home. Women, however, are being pulled in two directions at once, with cuts to benefits and mounting pressure on single parents to seek waged work forcing some women out of the home into the market place, while others are pushed back into the home through job losses and unemployment.

The Coalition government claims that cuts to public services - rather than tax increases - are the only answer to reducing the £156 billion fiscal deficit. These threatened public services can be seen as the state's contribution to the much wider category of social reproduction, particularly in the areas of care (child, social and health). All over the UK local authorities have begun to announce significant reductions of funding to social services, from libraries and healthcare to playgrounds and art groups, from rape crisis centres to domestic violence services. Of particular relevance to women are the profound effects that will be felt in children's services, both in council and community nurseries and in New Labour's flagship Sure Start Centres, which provide a variety of services to parents on a 'one-stop' basis. In Tower Hamlets, one of the poorest boroughs in Europe, £3m worth of cuts are being introduced to children's services alone in the financial year of 2011-2012, to be followed by a further £70m across the council in the next three years.[2]

Though services are withdrawn, the need for them remains, meaning that they must be provided elsewhere. The Coalition claims that they will be provided by the 'Big Society'. This is the government's fantasy that such services can be provided by the 'community' on an entirely voluntary basis. But behind this appropriated language of communalism and collectivity, the reality is that the withdrawal of state or publicly provided services means the privatisation of responsibility for social reproduction, away from the collective and 'the public' back onto to the individual. It is not speculative to assert that it will not be 'the community' - an amorphous, collective and undifferentiated common body - that will step in to provide these services. Evidence has shown repeatedly that in places where neoliberal projects of austerity have been rolled out, the bulk of the displaced responsibility falls on women.[3] Of course there is no single representative embodiment of 'woman': and women's varied experiences, and the contradictory intersections of constructions of 'womanhood' with those of 'race' and class, among others, mean that the cuts will not affect all women in the same way. We are not, as the government has claimed, 'all in this together'. Yet it remains true that women of all classes and ethnicities perform a disproportionately large part of unwaged reproductive labour in the home.[4] As such, it is women's burden of labour that is increased significantly through the withdrawal of state public services.

A second consequence of the austerity regime is to force women into the home by jeopardising their participation in the workplace outside the domestic sphere. Over a third of working women in the UK work in the public sector, from which 143,000 posts have disappeared in the year since the Coalition came to power.[5] Female - particularly youth - unemployment has reached the highest level in almost two decades, with almost half a million women currently claiming jobseekers allowance.[6] Meanwhile cuts to childcare, Disability Living Allowance, pensions and elder-care provision combine to make it increasingly difficult for women to balance waged work outside the home with the day-to-day work of caring for a house and the people who live in it.

There is, however, a contradiction here: as a result of cuts to benefits and the social wage, women are also being forced out of the home and into (predominantly low paid) waged work, as families increasingly require more income to cover the basic cost of living. Proposed benefit reform (closely resembling the 'workfare' programmes of the US) brutally promises to 'encourage' mothers back to work through compulsory labour programmes; lone parents will be expected to be actively seeking work when their children are as young as five years old.[7] The combined effects for working women of the removal of socially provided childcare (which should be seen as part of the social wage), the diminishing availability of work that pays an adequate wage, and the increase in their responsibilities for unpaid care work, tend to push women into informal labour markets, including sex work, that are unregulated, and in which workers face high levels of exploitation and, often, violence.[8]

The effects of all this are not only material; they also have an impact on our affective lives, and affect all the psycho-social elements of society; they make people less able to care for the emotional and intimate aspects of each other's lives - because of lack of time, energy and money - at the very moment in which they are in need of greater care. Again, it is typically women who are left to pick up the pieces. And on top of all this, these pressures are increasing at the exact moment in which mental health care provision is being demolished.

The current attack on social reproduction is only possible because of a long history of devaluing reproductive labour, constructing it as 'women's work', and accordingly rendering it invisible, and frequently unwaged or low-waged. It is this that allows the Con-Dem government to present services such as nurseries as 'non-statutory' luxury extras, which must simply be set aside when the time comes to tighten our belts. Shifting work into the home, where it is done 'for free', is a convenient way of hiding the hard realities of austerity behind closed doors.

Yet, though the government may hope that women will quietly mop up all the mess, the attack on social reproduction constitutes a serious economic, social and reproductive problem. *Someone* is still required to do the care work. In short, we are at risk of a widespread and potentially absolute crisis of care.

Feminist struggle: transformations of work and home

Feminists have long sought to claim the home as a politicised space, and the reproductive labour performed within it as real work. In the 1970s, the Women's Liberation Movement demanded state provision of '24 hour nurseries', to free mothers and carers from the home, and transform childcare outside the home into properly recognised waged-work. At the same time feminists organised *within* their homes, turning the domestic sphere into a terrain of struggle. Campaigns such as the National Childcare Campaign were an important impetus in institutionalising community nurseries, controlled by parents and workers and funded by the state.

Soundings

Much has changed since those early days of organisation. In the case of nurseries, for example, state support, whilst still grossly inadequate, has improved. But with increasing provision there has been an attendant increase in state regulation, and attempts to control ad hoc and informal childcare arrangements between women. And at the same time issues of childcare have become increasingly marginal to feminism, at both a theoretical and practical level. In this country at least, feminism has had a historically ambiguous and troubled relationship with the work of the home, and has at times been complicit in its devaluation. In particular, a liberal feminist focus on careerism and getting women into the upper echelons of management positions has involved an implicit debasement of non-market based female labour. Prominent public feminist campaigns of late, such as the Fawcett Society's 'Sexism and the City' 2008 manifesto, have focused on the gender 'pay gap', the workplace 'glass ceiling', and the fact that 'only 11% of FTSE 100 company directors are women' , as the main signifiers of gender inequality.[9] Of course alternative visions have been fought for, especially by working-class and/or women of colour; one of the most prominent and controversial of these has been the Wages for Housework campaign. Yet, at the moment it appears that a liberal individualist form of feminism, easily appropriated by and absorbed into capitalism, has won out, leaving the gendered division of labour in the home fundamentally unchallenged within dominant feminist discourses and movements.

Any feminist response to the austerity measures and their deeply gendered implications will, however, necessitate a re-focus on the home and the socially reproductive labour that takes place within it. One first step would be an assessment of what kind of political terrain 'the home' constitutes. And here - in the context of the increasing out-sourcing of reproductive labour, so that it becomes part of paid work, a commodity provided by poorer and often migrant women to higher-income women - we need to understand the power dynamics of the home in terms of race and class as well as gender. This analysis needs to locate the home within the matrix of waged and unwaged work that takes place both within and outside it.

Interestingly, despite the overlapping nature of their gendered roles as mothers, nursery workers, childminders or waged workers, women are frequently defined in highly oppositional terms. 'Successful career woman' versus 'stay at home mum' has become a tediously familiar motif of the mainstream media for at least the last forty years; and high levels of antagonism also exist at a more individual level between

Cuts are a feminist issue

'working mothers' and the women they pay to look after their children. The austerity measures may raise new issues about the perceived and real divisions that exist between women located within different constellations of class, labour market and home, but they are also likely to intensify and compound hostilities and existing inequalities.

The challenges of movement building: socialising care and the Big Society

It is clear that the sites and spaces of social reproduction - and the home in particular - are ones of struggle. The pressures of austerity may usher in an intensification of divisions between people, but they may also offer the possibilities of new and necessary alliances. The need to build links between workers and service users has resounded across the anti-cuts campaigns as they have begun to emerge in the UK, though thus far little attention has been paid to the processes by which this could come about.

An alliance between working mothers and childcare workers has radical potential. It would require - and therefore constitute - a significant shift in mentalities, thereby pushing against one of the key divisions from which capitalism has benefited. Bridging the distinction between waged/unwaged, productive/reproductive workers rejects the artificial distinctions between the two, while also confronting the very real issues which produce the divisions. This would not be an alliance to defend the current system, but to call for its transformation; for something better. Such alliances would also make visible the labour and economic impact of care work, confronting the logic at the heart of the government's representation of public services as a luxury extra.

But a feminist perspective on, and resistance to, the cuts should not be limited to overtly gendered issues such as childcare. Since the Con-Dem Coalition's spending review of October 2010, a number of new and important anti-cuts initiatives have emerged. Local anti-cuts campaigns across the UK acquired new energy and hope from the explosion of student protests in November and December, which also surely helped to make the TUC demonstration in March 2011 one of the biggest trade union marches in decades. Yet feminism remains somewhat marginal to such campaigns, with a disjuncture between all the proclamations about the sexist impact of the cuts and the grassroots forms of organisation that have emerged. A feminist approach to the cuts has to go further than simply asking for a more equitable distribution of the impacts of the cuts. For one of the problems with a liberal emphasis on the 'disproportionate' effects of the cuts on women (evidenced by the Fawcett Society's otherwise very interesting bid for a judicial review of the government's 2010 Emergency Budget) is that it implies that if only cuts were shared more equally between men and women, they would no longer be responsible for instituting further inequality. A few local anti-cuts campaigns are indeed beginning to highlight the cuts to children's services, and this is an important beginning. We need to move from here, however, to think about how to develop an approach that can account for the social stratifications that divide - as much as unite - women, and integrate it more fully into our grass roots organising, rather than simply ticking the box of gender equality.

Organising across these lines is complex and requires considerable amounts of work. Further complications lie in the fact that increasing women's unwaged working day often leaves them with little time for other activities, including political participation in collective organising. Feminist Fightback is currently at the very early stages of building links with other parents and service workers in the area of childcare, and of thinking about how to struggle collectively not only to defend existing children's services but also to create better ones. Such campaigns around childcare might be used as a starting point for building a much broader 'anti-cuts' movement that places at its centre questions of care, and the plurality yet connectedness of feminist demands.

Our thinking about the immediate problem of cuts to childcare has led us to more fully recognise the importance of care more broadly to the functioning and re-creation of communities. Our own movements for resistance and transformation also require significant amounts of reproductive labour, which is also often rendered invisible. As anti-capitalist feminists operating in the broader contexts of the left we have become increasingly alert to the amount of *work* done by activists in creating the bonds of trust and belonging that are so essential to building campaigns and collectives. While we do not wish to over-determine or essentialise the gender politics of this, our own experience has shown us that all too often - still - 'the boys' do the theory and 'the girls' do the practice (being friendly, organising social events, structuring participatory workshops). Both

Cuts are a feminist issue

forms of political work are crucial and need to be recognised as such: our task as feminists is to turn the revaluing of care inwards as well as outwards - to assert its importance within the social relations of our movement, as well as in the demands we make, and the battles we pick. How we look after each other becomes a question of even greater urgency as we face being evicted from homes and deprived of the resources required to maintain even a basic standard of living. If our movement is to sustain itself, it must be one that recognises the fragilities and dependencies that are being intensified by capitalism and the dramatic cuts; these should be seen not as weaknesses to be dismissed or overcome, but as suggestive of possibilities for new alliances and relations.

We have some idea what such a movement might look like - communal childcare, unemployed workers unions, food co-ops and housing collectives are only some of its more obvious manifestations. Many of these ways of organising are tools we are proud to have inherited from earlier generations of feminists; from Sylvia Pankhurst's East End nurseries at the turn of the twentieth century to the work of the WLM in the 1970s and the collective kitchens of Latin America. We are drawing on a feminist tradition of politicising questions of care and turning weaknesses and vulnerabilities into weapons and sources of power. But our aim is not simply to reproduce old patterns of resistance; we want to use previous insights to find our way through the present crisis. The 'home' is not the same place as it was thirty or forty years ago. The numbers of women with children in work are much higher, and the quantity of pre-school and nursery care has greatly increased. We have more single-parent families and more parents in gay relationships.

We are also responding to a different set of political circumstances, not least a different relationship between the family and the state. Our aim is for provision 'in and against the state'. This raises a core question in the struggle over public goods and shared resources and labour: how are we to ensure that our autonomous efforts to reproduce our own communities do not simply create Cameron's Big Society for him? - thereby endorsing the logic that if the state will no longer provide for us we will have to do it ourselves? This question remains utterly unresolved, both in theory and in practice. The answers, perhaps, will only be able to emerge through struggle, and must involve the possibility of using our unwaged labour not to enable capitalist accumulation but to create shared commons. Such commons may provide, for free, the necessary tasks of social reproduction - social care, child care, health, education -

not for the production of a new generation of workers to create profits, but to create a sphere within which human life is valued in and of itself - instead of solely for its contribution to the wealth of the few.

Socially reproductive work guarantees the possibility of life in capitalist society - and therefore of capitalism itself. The dramatic and brutal austerity measures introduced by the Con-Dem Coalition have shifted responsibility for this work from the state and public institutions to private individuals and families. Within this, it is largely women who step in as the state retreats at high speed, leaving behind a gaping chasm of care. It is women's unwaged labour that constitute the mythical 'Big Society' - which is one reason why is it is such a deeply gendered vision. Structural adjustment puts the simple task of sustaining life in danger.[10] This may be something around which we can organise: refusals to carry out reproductive labour have the power to stop the performance of capitalism itself. On the day of action on 30 June 2011, one of the biggest impacts of the public sector strikes was the 'problem' of how parents and carers would be able to look after their children when the schools were shut. Quite simply, without child care parents cannot work. Capital's accumulative strategies are stopped in their tracks. The cuts may be ideologically driven, but they are also messy and incoherent. And it is within these contradictions - working together across our identities as women, men, workers, public service users - that we may be able to carve out a different vision, instead of simply defending against savage attacks an imperfect liberal welfare state - one that is dependent on the exploitation of unwaged female labour.

This article is the result of ongoing conversations within Feminist Fightback and with other feminists and anti-cuts activists. Thanks are especially due to Camille Barbagallo and Silvia Federici, upon whose work we have drawn, and all those involved in Friends of Hackney Nurseries.

Feminist Fightback is a collective of self-defining women, developed out of conferences in 2006 and 2007. We're inspired by the politics of a range of anti-capitalist feminist struggles, and believe that no single oppression can be challenged in isolation. We are also committed to fighting for a feminist perspective and awareness of gender issues everywhere in our movement - and not marginalising 'women's rights' as a separate issue.

Cuts are a feminist issue

Notes

1. C.G. Caffentzis, 'On the notion of a crisis of social reproduction: a theoretical review', in Dalla Costa and Dalla Costa (eds), *Women, Development and Labor of Reproduction: Struggles and Movements*, Africa World Press 1999, p111.

2. Tower Hamlets Council, East End Life, 7.2.11: www.towerhamlets.gov.uk/news__events/east_end_life/7_february/what_council_cuts_will_mean_to.aspx.

3. H. Afshar and C. Dennis, *Women and Adjustment Policies in the Third World*, Macmillan 1992; and D. Elson and R. Pearson, 'The subordination of women and the internationalisaton of factory production', in Young, Wolkowitz and McCullagh (eds), *Of Marriage and Market: Women's Subordination Internationally and its Lessons*, Routledge 1981.

4. B. Anderson, *Doing the Dirty Work? The Global Politics of Domestic Labour*, Zed Books 2000.

5. B. Barber, 'Public sector job cuts hit women first', Guardian Online, 13.3.11: www.guardian.co.uk/commentisfree/2010/mar/13/public-sector-job-cuts-women.

6. H. Stewart, 'More women join dole queue as public sector cuts bite', 18.5.11: www.guardian.co.uk/society/2011/may/18/more-women-join-dole-queue-cuts.

7. From October 2011, parents will be denied income support and required to be actively seeking work in order to receive benefits: www://gingerbread.org.uk/news/127/100000-single-parents-to-be-cast-adrift-if-changes-to-job-seeking-reforms-not-delayed, accessed 16 Oct 2011.

8. Hardy and Sanders (forthcoming), 'The Political Economy of Lap Dancing: intersectional precarities and women's work in the stripping industry', *Work, Employment and Society*.

9. See Fawcett Society: www.fawcettsociety.org.uk/index.asp?PageID=630.

10. B. Young, 'Financial crises and social reproduction', in Bakker and Silvey (eds), *Beyond states and markets: the challenges of social reproduction*, Routledge 2008, p120.

Reviews

Generation wars

Craig Berry and Rhiannon Freeland

Ed Howker and Shiv Malik, *Jilted Generation: How Britain Bankrupted Its Youth*, Icon 2010

David Willets, *The Pinch: How the Baby Boomers Took Their Children's Future - and Why They Should Give It Back*, Atlantic 2010

As the post-war baby boomers approach retirement, there has been an explosion of interest in the financial and economic circumstances of different age cohorts, and more generally the relationships between different generations within society. This intellectual enterprise is, of course, not distinct from the experience of financial crisis and recession; the generational turn offers a unique perspective on - and even a partial explanation for - the country's economic woes.

The theme of both *Jilted Generation* and *The Pinch* is that the baby-boom generation - born between 1945 and 1965 - benefited from a fairly unique set of historical circumstances, and rather than seeking to share their good fortune with their children's generation, they have pulled the ladder up. Yet their conclusions are reached from very different starting points. Both books document the myriad problems today's young people will encounter in trying to find jobs, start families, get onto the housing ladder, or even simply 'have a say'; but whereas Howker and Malik concentrate on associating the ascent of the baby boomers with a very recent valorisation of individualism and unfettered free markets, Willets instead explains the apparent intergenerational theft orchestrated by the boomers with reference to social structures that are many centuries or even millennia old. For Willets, it is precisely the *size* of the boomer cohort that is to blame, not their politics.

Reviews

Jilted Generation's mission is to bust the myths surrounding the popular understanding of young people today. The reason that young people are struggling in the job market is not because of their inherent fecklessness but rather because of the drying up of opportunities. An examination of housing is the flagship contribution of *Jilted Generation* to the intergenerational relations debate, and it is hard to disagree with Howker and Malik's findings that the decline in construction, an increase in prices despite falling standards and sizes, the sale of public housing, and the end of tax relief for mortgage interest payments, have all combined to make buying a home a daunting and almost impossible prospect for many young people. This is exacerbated by the appalling state of the private rental market. Perhaps the most interesting aspect of the book, however, is Howker and Malik's treatise on the 'postponement of adulthood', a thread which features throughout. It is not simply that young people struggle to buy a house, find employment and start saving; more importantly, these struggles delay their attainment of full adulthood. This is something that may affect their entire lives, and moreover, may have an impact on society in general rather than simply the individuals directly affected. The increasing costs and declining value of higher education - which has become perhaps the defining issue of youth politics - is of course an important feature of *Jilted Generation*, but Howker and Malik are just as interested in the less privileged members of their generation, whose disadvantage has been compounded by an economy rigged in favour of the boomers.

Whereas Howker and Malik's inquiry invariably leads them to a left-wing critique of boomer politics, David Willets in contrast starts unambiguously from the right. He states boldly that baby boomers have failed to protect the interests of future generations, and indeed jeopardised future economic growth by failing to invest in infrastructure and control debt. One of the most interesting parts of *The Pinch* is a partial critique of 'discount rates' in economic theory, which encourage us to place little value in anything that may occur in a generation's time. However, according to Willets, Britain has never had strong intergenerational ties, owing to the fact that our nuclear families have always been small. Instead of patronage, we have created and relied upon commercial activity for sustenance, and civil society for social support. As in all human communities, family is crucial to our livelihoods and the source of our most meaningful experiences and relationships, but nevertheless our politics and economy reflect a relatively weak social contract between generations. It is precisely for this reason that when a large cohort such as the baby boomers comes

Soundings

along, it has the power to restructure culture, the labour market and the architecture of the state in accordance with its own immediate interest. While Willets documents the results of this 'pinch' expertly, he offers little by way of solutions, beyond a moderate plea for better education and advice for young people (including a slightly incongruous endorsement of free schools). He laments the declining importance of institutions (such as the family, but also universities, civil society organisations, nationhood, etc) that were stores of intergenerational wisdom, but merely asks that politicians consider more carefully the interests of the future rather than simply appealing to their present-day constituencies.

The empirical material amassed in both books is highly impressive, and both are extremely well-written. Yet there remains a sense that their generational approach obscures more than it explains. For Willets this is almost intentional. His main goal is to demonstrate that generational relations matter; in fact he argues that the intergenerational nature of human life has for too long been an under-appreciated determinant of fiscal and economic outcomes. In *Jilted Generation*, the focus on generational relations leads to an under-recognition of the class structure of the baby boomer cohort, and of the recessions in the 1980s and 1990s that brought poverty and hardship to so many of them during their working lives. It also leads Howker and Malik down some very awkward narrative paths, such as the suggestion that only funded pension schemes are intergenerationally fair, despite the profound consequences for pensioner poverty that could result when today's young people retire if the UK pensions system adopted a fully-funded model. Willets actually recognises the threat posed by the 'defined contribution' pensions that many young people will have to settle for, and in fact is more prepared than Howker and Malik to acknowledge intergenerational transfers from wealthy boomer parents as the genesis of inequality among today's young people - although he is clearly not uncomfortable with such outcomes, instead recognising them as a natural part of life.

Analysis and resistance

Michael Moran

David Beetham, *Unelected Oligarchy: Corporate and Financial Dominance in Britain's Democracy* Democratic Audit 2011 (www.democraticaudit.com/publications)

Democratic Audit has long been one of our most valuable sources in assessing the adequacy of democracy in the UK, and indeed elsewhere. It works by what might be called the technique of immanent critique: more simply, by just taking at face value the claims to democratic practice made by key institutions in the UK system, and asking the plain, but often devastating, question: do they live up to those claims? David Beetham has been one of the most important figures in the history of democratic audit, painstakingly pursuing the vocation of a true public intellectual: that is, a vocation that unites a commitment to serious research with a commitment to principled advocacy. *Unelected Oligarchy* is particularly timely. It appears at a moment when a key part of the business elite - finance - has recovered its confidence and its capacity to exercise influence following the blip that was the great financial crisis of 2007-8. Thirteen years of pro-business New Labour has been succeeded by a coalition whose two formally leading figures, David Cameron and Nick Clegg, are offspring of the City 'working rich'. The symbolism of that connection is matched by substance: they head an administration that is committed to responding to the crisis by a programme of public sector austerity and market deregulation.

Unelected Oligarchy, though, is only tangentially about our immediate condition. This is a study of the power of business in British politics. Business as a system of power has long lived in a tense marriage with democracy. But Beetham's case is that this tension has become more acute in the last three decades or so. He begins with a famous examination of the tension, Charles Lindblom's *Politics and Markets* (Basic 1977), which argued that property rules under a market economy, combined with the lobbying power of business, seriously circumscribed the decision-making capacity of the democratic state. Developments since then have further enlarged the power of business. Beetham documents the changes under four headings: the increasing dominance of free market ideologies; the rise of global corporations freed from the constraints of the nation state, coupled with the rise of financial intermediaries that have displaced productive functions by financial engineering; the increasing sophistication of the tax avoidance industry which allows corporations legally to escape their tax obligations; and the colonisation of public institutions themselves by corporate interests, in the guise of advisors, consultants and lobbyists.

This is superbly constructed in the finest tradition of radical argument based on serious inquiry. Moreover, in the best Democratic Audit tradition, it is presented with economy and exemplary clarity. Anyone who needs briefing on what has happened to corporate power in British democracy in the last generation need look no further.

Yet there is a strange silence here. Democratic Audit is an advocacy organisation with a distinguished history of arguing its corner; Beetham is one of the most distinguished examples of the tradition of the radical public intellectual, a figure often marginalised now in the world of professional social science. We might therefore expect some advocacy in this paper. Even Lindblom's gloomy account of a generation ago left slightly ajar the door for more effective regulation of the business enterprise by the democratic state. But the end point of Beetham's analysis is almost despair, or at least complete silence on what, if anything, might be done. Now Beetham might reply that a short paper cannot cover everything, and that his report is designed to sound the alarm bells about this unelected oligarchy, so that others might start thinking about how to curb it. But I also think there is something in the way the argument has been framed which leads to a kind of fatalism. Everything Beetham says about the forces underpinning the new power of business is convincing. But the traffic is not all one way, and only in a single grudging sentence about civil society critics ('strong civil society organisations have at best been able to generate embarrassment and achieve cosmetic changes') does he admit the existence of countervailing forces.

But these forces are surely more significant than Beetham allows; and because they are more significant there is more scope for action than he is prepared to envisage. Here are four examples. First, we can argue endlessly about the difference

Reviews

between a change of substance and a cosmetic change, but civil society organisations in the UK, notably in the public health domain, have had real success in beating back the power of big tobacco in the last generation. It has been hard, only partial, subject to circumvention, but the curbs on power have been real. Second, despite the rise of a market, pro-business ideology, business has found it increasingly hard to cash this: the evidence of opinion polls over a long time period now shows big business in particular has lost the battle for trust and approval among the population at large. Third, at the heart of the democratic state, the experience of political parties is more ambiguous than Beetham admits. He simply refers to inner-party democracy being 'stifled'; yet in all three leading Westminster parties the last generation has seen the growth of rank and file voice over candidate and leadership selection. Finally, while business has indeed colonised the state, the worlds of the public service - the conditions under which outsiders are appointed, the conditions under which contracts are awarded - are much more transparent and regulated, notably following our seventeen-year experience with the Committee on Standards in Public Life. None of these examples dents the main body of Beetham's argument. But dismissing the countervailing tendencies to corporate power has led him to a kind of fatalism. There is a lot to do to control this unelected oligarchy; but enough is being done to indicate that we need not despair.

A dubious appropriation

Alan O'Shea

Jesse Norman, *The Big Society*, University of Buckingham Press 2010

David Cameron first used the term 'the big society' publicly in a speech in November 2009: 'our alternative to big government is the big society. Social entrepreneurs and community activists already exist'; and, if this engagement were to spread across the population, 'we will have a national life expanded with meaning and mutual responsibility'. Cameron will have derived this notion to a large extent from the Policy Exchange think tank directed by Jesse Norman, and particularly the latter's book *Compassionate Conservatism* (2006). Norman has published two further books since, and sees *The Big Society* as drawing together this body of work.

It begins with a critique of New Labour, and habitual readers of *Soundings* will find many of his criticisms very familiar: its Fabian legacy of managerialist statism, turning citizens into passive consumers, and its (clumsy) micromanagement from above; Blair's centralisation of power to the clique around him; the failure to restrain risky speculation, or to tackle the housing crisis; and the highly regressive social decline that took place under New Labour, particularly for the young, the poor and ethnic minorities - bringing with it an increasing sense of powerlessness and lack of trust, a loss of values, and a growth of consumerism, alongside increases in drug use, binge drinking, teenage pregnancies and households without work. The underlying problem behind all this, Norman argues, is a 'consensus economics' that assumes that markets work via rational self interest - that individuals act independently of each other, on the basis of perfect information, to maximise their own gain or benefit. As he also argues, every aspect of this is false, and bears no relationship to messy reality: people are primarily social not economic animals - they act emotionally, ethically, with compassion, and make choices via a combination of

Reviews

factors, often not in their own economic interest. Furthermore, markets aren't always efficient (for example they mispriced credit), and are influenced by social contexts. There is also an interesting and useful section in the book that provides evidence of the negative impact of marketisation on the public sector, showing that imports from the private sector such as competitive appraisal, performance-related pay and target-setting are counter-productive: public sector workers are in general more concerned with the well-being of those in their care than with self-enrichment.

Norman therefore represents a clear break with Thatcherism and a return of 'society': here he draws on a Roman conception of society - a connected society of 'associates who collectively belong and recognise each other as belonging, a recognition that creates a mutual degree of respect and obligation between them'. The institutions which arise from these social relations 'build up a wisdom it is stupid to ignore'. His examples are friendly societies, which he celebrates as being run by the members for the members, 'so that costs were kept low and dishonest claims kept to a minimum'; these were 'sustained by a spirit of self-reliance and mutual support, which discouraged reliance on charity and state provision'; he also praises credit unions and the co-operative movement, which are seen as successful through 'self-help, entrepreneurship, and community energy - the virtues of Big Society - not state patronage and official intervention … and motivated as much by high ideals and a rich conception of human good as by economic necessity'.

Norman's appropriation of this tradition to Conservatism is unsurprisingly dubious. All the above institutions were of course formed by a working class struggling to survive in the face of exploitation and social exclusion, and were linked into the development of socialism, the foundation of the Labour Party and later the welfare state. But he argues that the Burkean tradition of Toryism has always respected the 'collective experience of previous generations', and particularly the 'wisdom of institutions', and has stressed 'trust, culture and tradition'. This tradition is 'unabashedly pro-market, but sees markets differently … neither controlling nor simply laissez-faire … pragmatic and non-ideological in character, a matter of instinct and judgement rather than the one-size-fits-all application of a political doctrine'. This approach gives it 'more freedom to act in accordance with simple common sense'. I don't need to elaborate how ideological all this is!

Norman proposes a 'leaner state'. The state is needed to contain the worst excesses of corporate power; to initiate a sovereign wealth bank to encourage economic long-termism; to deal with the problem of pensions and longevity; and to handle international relations - but not much else. There is only one small glimpse of an understanding that the big society needs a material base. His 'connected society' 'does not favour any particular section or group within society, except for supporting those in poverty, who may lack the capability to play a proper part in society at all, whether that lack is of cash, experience or opportunity'. But, while accepting the account of social malaise put forward in *The Spirit Level*, Norman does not take on the massive problem of inequality that this book points to. In the context of a very competitive capitalism forcing its way into every nook and cranny of society (including care of the elderly, the education of children, the health service), it is not possible to initiate or sustain the practices celebrated in the book without strong state effort at both national and local levels.

However, in his core argument Norman has pre-empted the left, 'Blue Labour', attempt to appropriate the values of 'tradition' and a rich 'connected' society sustained by mutual respect and compassion, and has enabled Cameron to outflank neoliberal New Labour as the 'compassionate' challenge; he has left the Labour leadership little room for manoeuvre until it is able to freely dissociate itself from its previous regime. But this restoration of 'society' to the political battleground can in the longer term be of great benefit to the left - though Ed Miliband's initial engagement via the theme of 'responsibility' is still a very thinned-out and rather punitive take on participative democracy. For Cameron's policies in relation to the Big Society are a gross travesty of what Norman is arguing - none of his 'new providers like charities, social enterprise, and private companies' are institutions run by the people for the people; nor do they offer any sign of user ownership and control, particularly in the light of the cuts in resources the government is making to two of the three. This gives Labour and the left more generally a big opportunity to reclaim the 'good sense' of Norman's account - mutualism, local control, and the prioritisation of well-being over market competition.

In sum, the book is an idiosyncratic weaving of elements into a sincerely-felt political perspective. But its own failings, and its cynical and selective reworking by Cameron, make it easy for the democratic left to re-appropriate this restoration of the individual as a social, collective and compassionate being into its own discourse. Having said that, neither left nor right seems to have noticed that the population at large has shown very little interest in the idea of such an enriched,

Reviews

more participative society. This is not surprising, given the long history that Norman outlines in which we have only been required to work, receive care and education and to consume. But people *are* very agitated by job insecurity, stress at work, over-long working hours, low pay, housing shortages, child care problems, and cuts to schools, hospitals and policing; and they are angry at the 'feral rich' as well as at the 'feral poor'. If we want to create the 'connected society' (which shares many features with the 'good society'), we might do better to centre a left movement on these urgently felt issues, only subsequently drawing in the deepening of democracy as the means to resolve them.

Craig Berry is a Senior Researcher at the International Longevity Centre-UK and former Policy Advisor at HM Treasury. His book *Globalisation and Ideology in Britain: Neoliberalism, Free Trade and the Global Economy* was published by Manchester University Press in 2011. **Rhiannon Freeland** is Operations Manager at the International Longevity Centre-UK and Parliamentary Assistant to Baroness Sally Greengross. **Michael Moran** is an adjunct professor at Manchester Business School and an affiliate of CRESC at the University of Manchester. His most recent publications include *Business, Politics and Society*, OUP 2009. **Alan O'Shea** is a former Professor of Cultural Studies at the University of East London and has written on Thatcherism and English modernity.

Relational economics

Andrea Westall

Recognising that economic life involves networks, connections and relationships is an important part of rethinking the economy.

———

There has been much discussion - in these pages and elsewhere - about the rise of excessive individualism and its impacts on our society and economy. Our economic system seems to 'prefer' and incentivise the more selfish and competitive aspects of our humanity. On the other hand we talk about the economy in terms of broad categories such as 'consumers' or the 'business community', or see it as subject to uncontrollable forces. But to discuss economics in terms either of isolated competing individuals or of abstract categories and forces is to ignore the role of people or the interactions and relationships between them. In the last issue of *Soundings*, Hilary Cottam talked about the need for 'relational welfare', arguing that in the current welfare system the power of money and transactions has overridden the importance of interactions and relationships between people. Similar issues and analysis are relevant to our economy: we also need a relational approach to economics.

Relational economics is useful in debates about how capitalism has become detached from political control, and in dealing with the more negative impacts of our economic system and ways of working on our personal, family and community lives. It can also aid thinking about how to deal with complex challenges that affect whole sectors and systems of economic activity, for example energy production and use.

There was a time, though, roughly from the mid-1990s, when people on the left spent time thinking about these issues. The focus then was on the increased effectiveness and productivity of more connected and relational ways of running local and regional economies, as well as the potential of 'new mutualism' to

Relational economics

recognise and reinforce the economic and personal benefits of joint activity. But those ideas were lost as New Labour was influenced by a pervasive neoliberalism, underpinned by a simplified form of neoclassical economics. That government generally pursued top-down economic policies, which mostly responded to individual businesses or entrepreneurs (except in relation to hi-tech, the 'knowledge' economy, or in struggling areas where the rules of 'normality' did not have to apply). Indeed, in the run up to the 2010 general election it was the Conservatives who seemed more receptive to this way of thinking, despite its roots in the left, and particularly in Labour's past.

However, such issues and concerns have been given more prominence by the financial crisis, as well as by a left emboldened by Labour's defeat to rethink fundamentals. Drawing particularly on the insights of Karl Polanyi, thinkers such as Maurice Glasman are engaging in a consideration of how more collaborative and relational ways of working could help people respond to and constrain large-scale economic power, restore morality or create forms of employee identity and security.[1]

Why do we have such difficulties in taking such ideas on board? What personal, cultural or systemic blockages disable us from thinking in this way? Why do practical examples showing that collaboration and co-operation are effective (even when there is strong evidence of positive benefits) receive so little attention - or remain 'unheard', on the margins, seen as 'exceptional'? We need to spend time reflecting on, and removing, such blockages - otherwise we will not be able to change the dominant common sense. And alternative ideas, policies or plans could fail again. Stuart Hall and Doreen Massey explain this inability to entertain alternatives partly in terms of the way that dominant ideas have become embedded within our common sense.[2] As Tony Judt has said, part of 'our disability is discursive'.[3]

The aim of this article is to draw attention to the implications and possibilities of focusing on relationships between people and businesses in the economy, and to spark discussion on the many and varied blockages to thinking and acting in this way.

Examples of a more relational approach

We first need to remind ourselves (yet again) that economic and market activity have always worked through norms and human relationships. Different motivations

Soundings

(including collaboration, competition and negotiation), codes of behaviour, intermediaries, government, and forms of civil society, have always been part of containing and balancing excesses, or attempts by businesses to break away and prioritise self-seeking behaviour. It is a mark of our currently limited ways of thinking that we even need to say this - so used are we to talking of 'the market', or feeling powerless in the face of seemingly uncontrollable, hard to understand and abstract 'forces' of globalisation or finance. But our feelings of impotence partly stem precisely from the weakening of these connections.

There is, of course, more to relational economics than just a focus on individual and business relationships. For example, the behaviour of systems with many players can be 'emergent' (in other words, different from the sum of individual actions). Complex feedbacks or reinforcements, institutional and policy changes, technological shifts, and the increasing scale and scope of economic activity, have all led to systems that seem beyond capture, understanding and control. But this complexity points to a need to try to understand connections rather than to retreat yet again into abstraction and equations.

A focus on relationships or connections between people, economic organisations and political processes opens up possibilities for thinking in different ways about a wide range of contemporary issues - for example in thinking about how to re-embed economic activity within political oversight and engagement (such as through forms of diverse and multi-stakeholder economic networks at local, regional or sectoral level); or about how to reduce the more negative impacts of our economy on personal, family or community lives (for example through joint childcare facilities between small businesses in an area, or through homeworkers forming groups to reduce exploitation and isolation); or about how to address complex challenges (for example through creating appropriate cross-sectoral networks to effect system change in areas such as energy, or through organisations sharing their resources). Relational thinking can also assist in finding new ways to re-empower people or rebalance power (for example through networks or unions of the self-employed to enable effective voice and action, or to provide collective and cheaper services); or new ways to restore morality and ethics (for example, through peer groups in the economy with codes of practice); or it can assist in providing identity and points of security (again through forms of mutual economic support). It can also help to increase effectiveness and productivity (for example diverse multi-stakeholder

Relational economics

groups and networks can enable decision-making, 'distributed' production, information sharing, or innovation).

It may be helpful at this point to look in more detail at a few areas, particularly those which are often ignored by the left. One such area is that of small business and self-employment, which account for roughly half of employment and half the value of the economy. (The left often seems more comfortable focusing on large-scale corporate behaviour, perhaps because of its historical focus on worker solidarity and action.)

The self-employed (admittedly a group that is hard to define and difficult to measure) merge confusingly into employment, and are extremely diverse and under-researched. They are therefore liable to be misunderstood and dealt with by blunt policy instruments. What we do hear tends to be partial - for example, the exaggerated flexibility and job satisfaction of the knowledge-based freelancer, or the exploited and forcibly self-employed construction worker. (The last government tried to tackle some of the problems of the latter with legislation, which, because it was top-down and 'one-size-fits-all', also managed to negatively hit the former.) We hear from talking to people, anecdotes, and a few studies, that the benefits of working at home for some (for those employed, self-employed or somewhere in the middle) can turn into isolation. Or that the self-employed can find themselves at a disadvantage against the power of larger businesses - whether from, say, disproportionately expensive insurance, late payment practices, or wasteful purchasing of individual resources that are rarely used.

Solutions based on co-operation do exist. Examples include self-employed people coming together to negotiate more favourable terms and provide services - some as part of unions (like the National Union of Journalists), others organised independently. And some sectors have long histories of sharing resources (such as co-operative machine rings in agriculture). But some people are too scared to challenge the status quo, or too isolated to create more beneficial ways of working together. We could therefore think a lot more about how groups of self-employed people (or isolated homeworkers) could share resources and link up. Some of the self-employed have expressed the desire for forms of collective power, which may also provide services. The Self-Employed Women's Association in India, for example, shows the potential of organising together through union activity for those who are least able to spontaneously create such networks.[4] And this issue could also create a more engaged role for political activity. Local councillors or MPs could help facilitate networks of homeworkers and the self-employed, opening up underused public spaces, or encouraging the use of shared resources; or the creation of collective goods, assets and services, such as childcare.

Relational thinking is also extremely helpful in thinking about regulation. Calls for tougher regulation and limits abound in finance, after the perceived weakness of self-regulation or monitoring bodies such as the Financial Services Authority. But it is well known that regulation has to be implemented, internalised and action scrutinised, to be truly part of changing behaviour. We often pit government legislation (strong, but with dangers of being blunt) against self-regulation (engaged, but with dangers of 'we-think') without realising that we should be focusing more on creating what Peter Grobovsky has described as 'layered webs of regulatory influence'.[5]

Or what about the role of relationships in more complex economic situations, whether in particular geographical areas, or sectors or systems within the economy? Think about how relational thinking could contribute to considering ways to embed the economy in negotiated commitments, enabling the creation of shared values or increasing resilience and sustainable productivity. Paul Hirst's work on associative democracy is invaluable here, in terms of thinking about extending economic governance throughout the economy, developing the role of relationships between employees, or opening up forms of corporate governance to more stakeholder models.[6] Thus, for example, Penny Shepherd has drawn on examples from finance to show how links between people with similar roles and jobs can be used to reinforce or create codes of ethics or norms of behaviour - thereby reducing the potential for isolated people to behave in an individual and unethical way.[7]

Such approaches require interventions and co-operation at many levels: the Future Foundation has looked at encouraging system innovation by working with relevant players to 'transform the key systems that underpin human activity - like food, energy and finance - to make them more resilient, equitable and sustainable for the future'; and intermediaries like the Marine Stewardship Council have become market-changers by setting standards in co-operation with industry members.[8] Examples like these involve relationships between people or businesses that might be similar or different. They also raise a host of practical challenges. For example, do we have the personal or work experiences to enable us to behave in a robust and

Relational economics

respectful way, rather than through conflict or reluctant consensus? Our behaviour often seems to mirror our polarised language of collaboration versus competition. But difficult and robust negotiation will be necessary to transform and shift complex systems, create resilient local economies, or balance different power interests.

There are, of course, limits. For example, a focus on relationships between people and stakeholder groups does not necessarily address or enable us to incorporate wider public interests, those of future generations or environmental limits.

Some of the blockages that prevent us hearing or acting

Responses to our increasing sense of isolation and the growth of individualism have varied widely. The Coalition's Big Society is a response to perceived problems within the welfare state, or society more generally; the left tends to blame Thatcher and neoliberalism. The reasons are many and varied, contested, and likely to be self-reinforcing. As Doreen Massey and Stuart Hall pointed out, they reach back into our past, and come from societal as well as political changes, and from both the left and the right.[9]

Academic and business language

There are many reasons why neoclassical economics has taken hold of our everyday thinking. And by doing so, it has itself influenced reality, despite its known limitations. One of the most important issues for this discussion is that it is capable of being presented in easily simplified terms; and its powerful proponents have a strong belief in, and promotion of, its widespread applicability.

The neoclassical model appears to be based on human behaviour, in its assumption of the rational and individual 'man' who makes decisions through rational self interest. Of course, 'mainstream' economics has itself become more complex and nuanced, despite retaining these individual assumptions. Behavioural economics, for example, the political flavour of the month, seeks to incorporate how people actually behave - partly informing 'Nudge'-based policies. But this approach is still predominantly individualistic and asocial. The role of norms, and sanctions, and the way in which our behaviour changes as we become 'other-regarding' in

Soundings

group situations, is not easily accommodated. Less popular attention has been given to the implications of another mainstream economic assumption, that of isolated businesses that interact with individual customers. The reality, as we know, is far more complex.

The 2009 Nobel Prize in Economics, however, went to Elinor Ostrom - a political economist who draws on institutional economics and anthropological insights in her work, for example on the governance and management of common resources. From in-depth studies of real-world systems, and the messy and overlapping interactions between people and institutions, she shows how expert top-down control is not as effective as having many sites of group decision-making. Contrary to most policy approaches, and Hardin's 'Problem of the Commons', people can actually be very good at designing their own rules and sanctions. This kind of more 'realistic' and relational approach and analysis needs to be further developed within economic policymaking.

Unfortunately, the old school continues to dominate within the establishment, and a simplified version of neoclassical economics has taken hold of much policy development and theory. Despite ongoing criticism, there seems to be little effort, in research or practice, to create new frames for policy development, or to address and counter underlying assumptions and rationales. A pervasive example of this lack of critical thinking is the way in which 'market failure' persists as the dominant rationale for government policy. While it is also tempered by other factors - and is often a *post hoc* validation for the more idiosyncratic or political predilections of ministers - it subtly affects much of what is done. Consider, for example, the linguistic implications of the primacy of markets. If the state can only respond to 'failure', this reduces or inhibits its ability to be transformatory - in other words to attempt to change the rules of entire economic or market activities.

The experience of the co-operative movement is illustrative. Under a rebadging or reframing of 'social enterprise', to fit with the dominant language of New Labour, they, and other forms of alternative business models, were recognised by the then Department for Trade and Industry. But, partly because of the overlaps with the charity and voluntary sectors, the focus on alternative business structures was mostly ignored and relegated to dealing with 'market failures', particularly in 'deprived' local areas.

The related idea of 'externalities' (side effects of economic activities that aren't

Relational economics

reflected in the cost, for example, pollution) has mostly led to policy solutions which focus on individual businesses, for example through financial incentives such as taxation or specific grants, or through exhortation to forms of internal corporate social responsibility. Other business 'truisms' also persist, despite examples and evidence to the contrary: for example the belief in inevitable business efficiency, or in the power of contracted relations to better deliver outcomes, or the supremacy of the shareholder model. And business language such as 'win-win' hides the reality of different trade-offs and power differences between people.

The cultural reinforcement of individual economic behaviour

National business cultures, influenced by the specificities of national history, undoubtedly play a role in economic behaviour. For example many observers argue that UK businesses or individuals are relatively less inclined towards collaborative behaviour than others in Europe. Back in the 1990s, when talk of mutual guarantee schemes, small business networks and distributed or connected economies were being discussed, there were many comments along the lines of 'But it won't work here'. Recently, while doing some work on agricultural co-operation across the EU, I was told that in Britain (particularly in England, and in certain subsectors), farmers and other agricultural producers were considered relatively reluctant to work with others. One reason for this that was mooted by several people was that the side effects of top-down government collective action (for example through the Milk Marketing Board) have been to reduce the more spontaneous development of mutually beneficial relations between farmers. Whatever the widespread validity of this claim, it is likely that such reluctance is likely to be historically contingent, and to be related to other areas as well as farming. People in Britain also seem to be more likely to see the world in terms of binary opposition - for example, competition versus collaboration.

Blockages from the left

It is too easy to place all the blame for this individualistic and economic approach on rampant neoliberalism, large disembodied corporate bodies, or the financial system. But, as Stuart Hall points out, where we are is also the result of actions fought for by the left. Fabian (and Marxist) inspired policies that abstract and aggregate economic realities are also part of the problem. Much of the Fabian approach, and also that of social democracy more generally, has focused on growth, which can then be redistributed to those less fortunate. Recent debates about social democracy are seeking to rethink the flaws in this particular framing, to open up discussions about the nature of growth, the implications for the role of the state, and the arguments for pluralising business models and motivations.

Thinking and practice around an economy which focuses more on relationships between people (whether for self-interest, solidarity, equating equalising power relations or problem-solving) has its roots in a more bottom-up, utopian, co-operative or guild socialism. The left generally seems to have forgotten this, preferring top-down solutions in preference to an alternative that is sometimes dismissed as a partial, exclusive or a smothering form of communitarianism.

Part of the problem again relates to lazy thinking in binary opposites - left-right; confrontation-consensus, capital-labour. A more transformational economic policy will need to transcend this tendency to simple opposition, and recognise the importance of a greater balance of co-operation and collaboration throughout the economy.

It will also need to quickly work through the blockages that contribute to our pervasive inability to fully accommodate environmental and 'future' issues into economic thinking. For some, the wished for nirvana is a technological fix that will sort out any major environmental problems. But, though technology will obviously be part of the solution, the substantial changes, opportunities and disruptions that will also be necessary pose profound challenges for democratic decision-making, requiring new forums and spaces for such discussions, as well as ways to take future concerns into account.[10]

And there also seems to be a more general reluctance or difficulty on the left in discussing the economy: relevant debates seem only to occur between a relatively small pool of 'experts'. So another blockage might be a lack of real engagement by enough people in understanding and debating the economy, and its links with society and culture.

Some ways forward

Our over-individualised habits of thought and experience, fear of complexity, limited

Relational economics

language, as well as social-democratic or broader left mantras or framings (not just neoliberal), all contribute to preventing us from seeing the relevance and importance of people's relationships in the economy. But such an understanding is important for increasing resilience and productivity; for improving individual wellbeing and the work-life balance; for addressing wider challenges (especially environmental); and for finding ways to get a better hold on the economy, and subjecting our actions to more considered political and democratic decision-making and control. We might think, for example, about how multi-stakeholder spaces for decision-making and action could be part of enabling appropriate and timely changes in different sectors. Or how the primacy of economic and business language needs to give way to more human ways of speaking about, designing, legitimising and impacting on economic policy. We could also consider how individuals who do similar jobs across the economy might better use and create codes of behaviour that provide solidarity and touchstones to 'do the right thing'.

And Labour Party members, others on the left and political thinkers more widely need to become much more economically literate, not just through simple economic training (itself part of the problem) but through understanding the wider ways in which we can think about and structure our economic reality. We might also need to think about how we can better develop experiences and skills which enable us to work with different people and organisations to create shared values and agreed ways forward. Perhaps there could be more learning about how to negotiate and deliberate in schools, as an alternative to the current very often simplistic debates (where they have them), which tend to mirror a competitive or conflictual economy, politics and legal system.

But let's not get too carried away, and start seeing relational, connected or distributed economies as the next big thing. We have often failed in the past, through extending the latest insights or fashions beyond their relevance. These approaches are contingent and specific, partial, and definitely not 'one-size-fits-all'. And none of this will enable us to address environmental constraints and intergenerational equity, if we focus solely on relations between people alive today. Tbc …

Andrea Westall is a writer, Visiting Senior Research Fellow at the Open University, and a Strategy and Policy Consultant. She is editor of *Revisiting Associative Democracy*: www.lwbooks.co.uk/ebooks/AssociativeDemocracy.html.

Soundings

Notes

1. See for example Maurice Glasman et al (eds), *The Labour Tradition and the Politics of Paradox*, www.lwbooks.co.uk/ebooks/labour_tradition_politics_paradox.html; Karl Polanyi, *The Great Transformation*, Rinehart 1944.

2. For example in Stuart Hall 'The Neoliberal Revolution' and Doreen Massey 'Economics and ideology in the present moment', in *Soundings* 48.

3. Tony Judt, *Ill fares the land*, Penguin 2010.

4. See www.sewa.org.

5. Peter Grabosky, 'Using non-governmental resources to foster regulatory compliance', *Governance: an international journal of policy and administration* 8 (4), 1995.

6. Some of these ideas were explored, criticised and extended at *Revisiting Associative Democracy*, a seminar organised in 2010, and an ebook of the same name, (ed. Andrea Westall), published by Lawrence & Wishart in 2011: www.lwbooks.co.uk/ebooks/AssociativeDemocracy.html.

7. Penny Shepherd, 'The case of capital markets', in *Revisiting Associative Democracy*.

8. See http://www.futurefoundation.net/; www.forumforthefuture.org/blog/what-system-innovation; www.msc.org; Philipp Schepelmann, *Ecological Industrial Policy for Ecological Structural Change*, Friedrich Ebert Foundation 2011.

9. See their articles in *Soundings* 48, full reference in note 3.

10. One organisation that is trying to reconcile the tensions and conflicts between environmental concerns and democracy, is the Foundation for Democracy and Sustainable Development www.fdsd.org.

Where did it all go wrong for George Osborne?

Michael Burke

It is the government's policies that are causing economic stagnation, not the wider economic crisis.

———

The depression of the British economy is not a unique event: two other large economies in the European Union are also in a depression. The performance of this group of three countries (the others are Italy and Spain) is in contrast to a number of EU countries that have (nearly) recovered the total loss of output incurred in the course of the recession. This group includes Sweden, which has recovered all the lost output of the recession; Germany, which is back to it pre-recession peak; and to a lesser extent France, which is still 0.8 per cent below its own prior peak in output. A third group consists of economies that have been the subject of 'bail-outs' by the Troika of the EU/ECB/IMF. If not beforehand, then since the imposition of deep public spending cuts, Greece, Ireland and Portugal have experienced very deep domestic recessions. The economies in the intermediate grouping of Britain, Italy and Spain are all effectively stagnating. The GDP data for the second quarter of 2011 show that the British economy grew cumulatively by just 0.1 per cent in the three quarters since the Comprehensive Spending Review, while Italy and Spain grew by 0.5 per cent and 0.7 per cent respectively.

However only in Britain was this stagnation a matter of domestic political choice.

Soundings

Policy choices and stagnation

Of the three large stagnating economies, Spain had a much milder recession than either Britain or Italy. Spanish GDP contracted by a severe 4.9 per cent in the course of the recession, but this was exceeded by both Britain and Italy, which experienced contractions of 7.1 per cent and 6.9 per cent respectively, despite the fact that neither British nor Italian policy-makers had to cope with any problems on the scale of Spain's debt-fuelled construction boom.

The reason for the less severe downturn in Spain, despite arguably worse circumstances, is that the initial response of the Spanish government was the most effective of any of the leading European economies in combating recession. While the scale of the initial stimulus measures was only slightly above the EU average of 2 per cent of GDP, Madrid overwhelmingly concentrated its stimulus on public investment, especially in infrastructure projects. These are widely and authoritatively recognised as producing the most effective bang for buck in terms of government spending (technically speaking, they have by far the largest fiscal multipliers attached).[1] In addition, at no fiscal cost at all, the minimum wage was raised - and transfers to the poor are regarded as the next most effective means of stimulating the economy, since the poor are obliged to spend by far the greater proportion of their incomes (in Keynesian terms, the poor have the greatest marginal propensity to consume).

As a result, the recession was less severe in Spain, even though its construction boom had been far greater: in the years 1997 to 2007, investment in Spanish construction expanded by 90 per cent in real terms, nearly twice the rate of the economy as a whole; by contrast the British construction boom saw an expansion of 50 per cent, and growth in Italian construction over the same period was a much more modest 26 per cent.

Prospective recovery has been halted in Spain, however, because of a combination of actions by financial markets, ratings agencies and the European Central Bank, which together conspired to drag Spain into the debt crisis. The initial actions of Spain's socialist government were enough to cushion the effects of the recession. But its subsequent capitulation to the pressures for a bail-out of its creditors and the accompanying cuts to public spending have since consigned it to the economic doldrums.

Italy represents an altogether different case. Italy is the Japan of Europe. While

Where did it all go wrong for George Osborne?

Japan is now widely described as having lost decades in the form of negligible growth since 1990, Italy's economic performance has been marginally worse over that period. Italian GDP has grown by just 20 per cent since 1990, 0.6 per cent less than Japan in real purchasing power parity terms, and much less than the British economy's 48 per cent growth. The severity of the Italian recession is not a function of a preceding boom - there wasn't one. Instead it is a function of structural weakness exacerbated by a political leadership which is far more interested in keeping out of jail and attacking foreigners than in resolving the crisis.

The first Italian 'austerity' measures have only recently been announced, and are yet to be implemented. Italy was caught up in the generalised crisis and responded in the now customary European fashion with a reduction in government spending, even though the public sector deficit had already fallen to below pre-recessionary levels. When the measures are enacted, the current period of economic stagnation may come to be regarded fondly as a growth interlude, as the economy responds negatively to the withdrawal of government spending. In common with the Euro area as a whole, Italian government spending accounts for approximately half of GDP. As will be discussed below, it is a fallacy to believe that other agents, consumers or businesses will expand their own spending in response. Households will be directly hit by cuts in public sector wages, benefits and services; while expecting business to increase their investment under those circumstances is foolish in the extreme.

By contrast to Spain, where external agents forced a turn towards spending cuts, and Italy, which is in long-term stagnation, Britain was in recovery mode when the current government took office. It is worth emphasising this point, not least because George Osborne's explanation for what the Office of National Statistics calls 'flatlining' is that the Tory-led coalition government inherited an economy in recession when they came into office. This is wholly factually incorrect.

As Figure 1 below shows, the British economy had been expanding moderately until the Coalition government took office, and had been making up lost ground on the Eurozone economy. It has been diverging from Eurozone growth since the Tory economic policies were implemented. Taken together, the economy expanded by 2.8 per cent over the course of five quarters that began in the third quarter of 2009 and ended with the third quarter of 2010. Uniquely, Osborne inherited a moderate but sustained recovery. It is the policies adopted since which have produced stagnation.

No external agency has obliged the government to adopt this course, and indeed

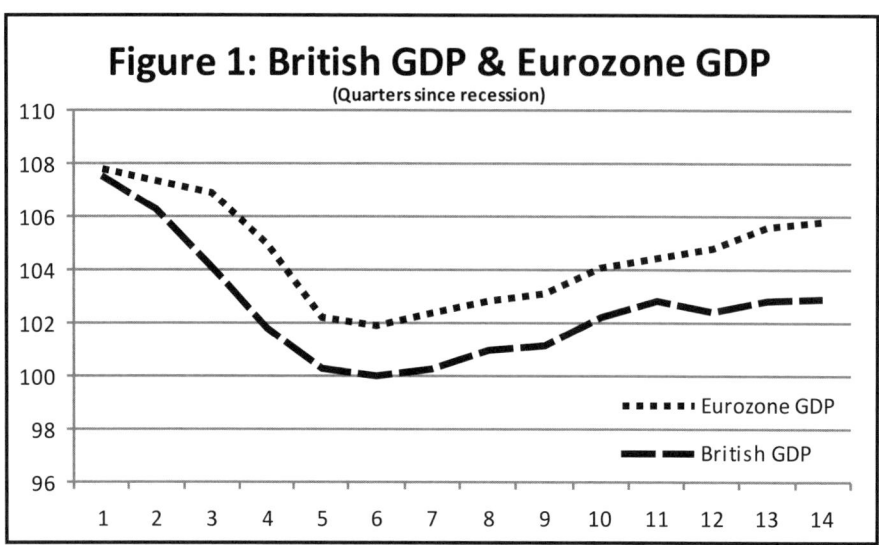

Figure 1: British GDP & Eurozone GDP (Quarters since recession)

many seasoned economic commentators - such as Martin Wolf of the *Financial Times* - have cautioned against it. There has been no imposition of cuts from the EU, acting in concert with the ECB, as occurred in Spain. Nor was Britain panicked into a policy because of its place in a general European-wide contagion, as Italy has been.

It is sometimes argued that the policy was pre-emptive, in that it forestalled a bond market crisis that would have otherwise occurred. In a similar way to the Chancellor's focus on the elusive 'structural deficit' rather than the actual deficit, this claim is designed to prevent conclusive debate, since by its nature it is not possible to disprove it on the basis of empirical evidence.

But the argument is nevertheless demonstrably false. The Labour budget of March 2009 provided a significant stimulus to the economy (though slightly below the EU average), equivalent to 2 per cent of GDP. Yet in the year following this increase in government spending, the real yield on benchmark gilts was unchanged, and remained close to zero. In other words, a significant stimulus led to no increase in borrowing costs. There was no imminent bond market crisis to address.

Policies leading to stagnation

There are two main levers in formulating economic policy - fiscal and monetary policy. British monetary policy is in the hands of the Bank of England, and was

Where did it all go wrong for George Osborne?

unchanged throughout the period between the two Labour budgets of March 2009 and March 2010. Monetary conditions were also broadly unchanged. As we have seen, real long-term interest rates were unaltered, while sterling's trade-weighted index mostly appreciated over that period (thus producing a moderate headwind against recovery), but ended more or less where it started.

The recent sharp deterioration in economic outlook and performance must be a function of a change in fiscal policy alone, as monetary policy has continued to be more supportive, via unchanged base rates, 'Quantitative Easing' and a lower exchange rate for the pound. And the main change in policy implementation arose after the Coalition government took office in May 2010: in June 2010 it announced an 'emergency budget', which was soon followed by a much more thoroughgoing attack on public spending in the October Comprehensive Spending Review. The net effects of these changes can be seen in the Treasury Budget table set out below in Figure 2 (taken from the March 2011 budget). They show the net fiscal tightening under the Coalition government as £9.4bn in the last financial year (of which £5.5bn is spending cuts and £3.8bn is tax increases). This proposed fiscal tightening rises to £41bn in the current financial year.

At the time of writing, the financial year April 2010 to March 2011 has only recently ended. The financial year 2011-12 is just a few months old. Therefore the impact of the cuts that has been seen to date relates much more to the £9.4bn of spending cuts and tax increases from the financial year 2010-11 than to the much larger £41bn fiscal adjustment in the financial year 2011-12. Disentangling monthly government accounts is not a simple task, but the best guess is that the first three months of the financial year 2011-12 account for a scheduled one quarter of the

Figure 2 Total consolidation plans over the forecast period

£ billion

	2010-11	2011-12	2012-13	2013-14	2014-15	2015-16
Policy Inherited by the Government	1	26	41	58	72	
Spending	0	14	25	39	51	
Tax	1	12	16	19	21	
Spending share of consolidation (per cent)	0	54	61	67	71	
Total discretionary consolidation	9.4	41	61	88	110	126
Spending	5.5	22	38	59	80	95
Tax	3.8	20	23	29	30	30
Spending share of consolidation (per cent)	59	53	62	67	73	76

Source: Treasury, Budget 2011

The top half of the table shows proposed Labour fiscal tightening ('consolidation') in their March 2010 budget, and the bottom half the Coalition government revision.

total fiscal consolidation for the year, or approximately £10bn. But even these data do not reflect the full proportion of the effect of the cuts. This is because economies respond with a time lag to changes in economic policy. (Alan Greenspan used to say that this time lag was 'long and variable', providing the ultimate get-out clause for policy-makers. But though the former Fed Governor may have wanted too much leeway, there is clearly some lapse in time between policy change and economic impact.) This means that, since the £10bn in cuts of the first quarter of the financial year 2011-12 is contemporaneous with the second quarter of GDP data, they can hardly be said to have affected it. Therefore the transition from recovery to stagnation during this period can be seen as almost entirely a reflection of the earlier £9.4bn in fiscal tightening.

The crisis of private sector investment

The British economy has undergone a zig-zag - boom, recession, recovery, stagnation. But during all the period following the boom there has been a single constant - the crisis of private sector investment. The peak of the last business cycle was in the first quarter of 2008, and the trough of the recession was in the second quarter of 2009. Over that time the economy contracted by £88.6bn in real terms, on an annualised basis.

This fall in GDP can be broken down into its main components. Thus household consumption fell by £41.5bn, a drop of 4.9 per cent - one of the biggest percentage declines of the major economies. In the OECD as a whole the fall in household consumption was a much more modest 1.5 per cent. (This suggests that the social safety net in Britain is both too weak and too porous.) By contrast, government current spending rose by £7.4bn. Net exports also rose, making a positive contribution to growth of £16.4bn during the recession, but this was entirely a function of collapsing demand for imports, which outstripped the fall in exports. Investment (gross fixed capital formation), however, fell by £43bn. The private sector is in fact responsible for a decline of £51.1bn, because the total figure for investment also includes government investment, which expanded during the recession by £8.1bn. This means that, out of a total decline in GDP of £88.6bn, the decline in private sector investment accounts for £51.1bn, or 57.7 per cent of the total. These main aggregates of the national accounts in the

Where did it all go wrong for George Osborne?

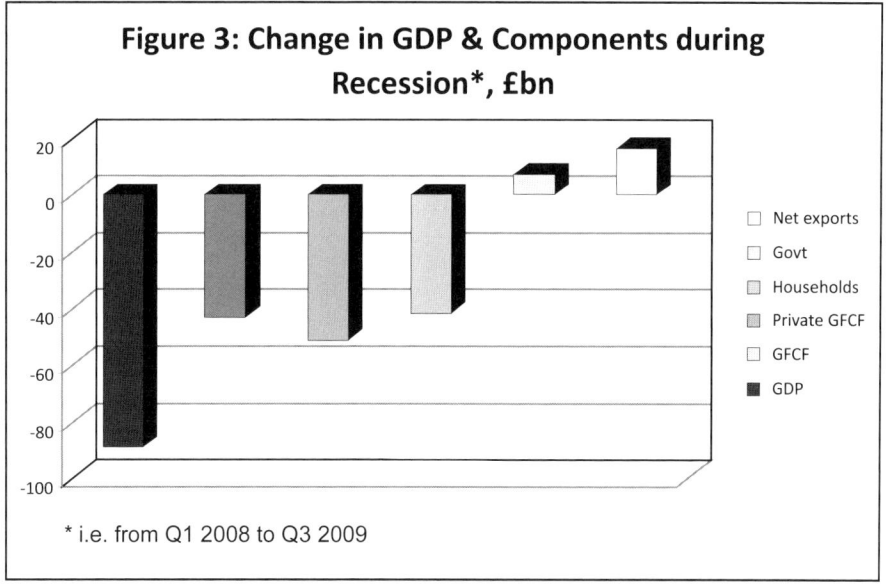

recession are shown in Figure 3 above.

Despite a recovery that began in the fourth quarter of 2009, the level of GDP remains well below its peak of the first quarter of 2008. At the end of the first quarter of 2011 GDP was still £56.3bn below the peak level three years earlier, a shortfall of 4.1 per cent (detailed data are not available for the second quarter at the time of writing). Household consumption has recovered to some extent, so that at the time of writing it is £36bn below its peak level. Government current expenditure and net exports have both risen, by £13bn and £17.3bn respectively. But investment has resumed its decline in the last two quarters. It is now £36.1bn below its peak, a figure that is fractionally worse than the fall in household consumption. The private sector is in fact responsible for a £44.9bn decline in investment, but this has been offset by government investment, which has risen by £8.8bn. This private sector investment strike thus accounts for £44.9bn of a total loss of output of £56.3bn - 79.8 per cent of the total. The main aggregates of the national accounts from the end of the boom to the first quarter of 2010 are shown in Figure 4 below.

Cause of recovery

As previously stated, recovery began in the fourth quarter of 2009 and lasted for

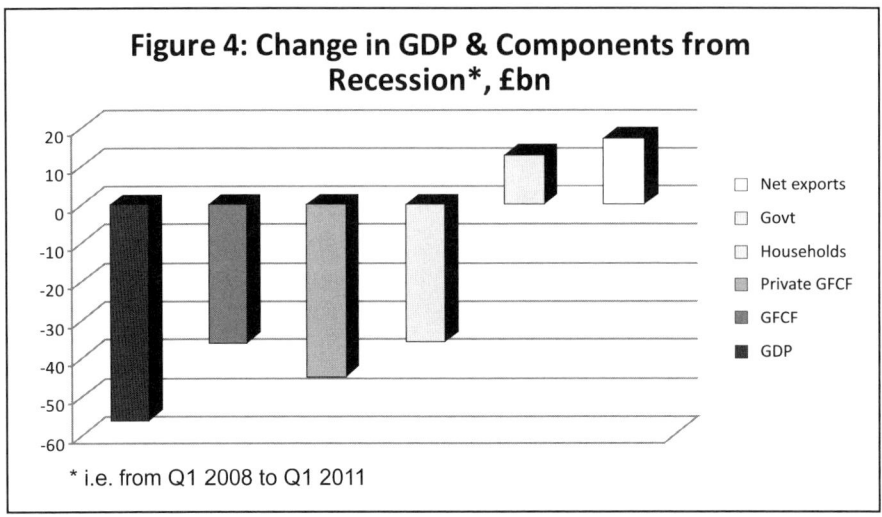

four quarters, with the economy expanding by £32.8bn. During these four quarters household consumption rose by £11.7bn, up 1.4 per cent; net exports fell by £12.6bn; government current spending rose by £3.8bn; and investment rose by £12.5bn. The private sector contribution to this increase was £15bn, as government investment fell over the period as a whole, once the impact was felt of the new government's policies.

These figures may have encouraged the government and the Office for Budget Responsibility in the false idea that the recovery would be driven by investment even as government spending was cut. (The other officially projected component of growth is net exports, but, as noted, the rise in net exports currently remains entirely a function of the slump in import demand. British exports in the first quarter of 2011 remained below their pre-recession peak, despite the sharp rebound in world trade.) Thus the Office for Budget Responsibility forecast in March 2011 that private investment would rise by 6.7 per cent during the financial year. The reality is that it is currently moving in the opposite direction: in the first quarter private sector investment fell by 3.8 per cent from the final quarter of 2010.

To understand why the government and Office for Budget Responsibility have been proved wrong in projecting higher private sector investment, the dynamic underlying the recovery and subsequent stagnation must be examined. This can be understood through looking at Figure 5, which shows the trends in

Where did it all go wrong for George Osborne?

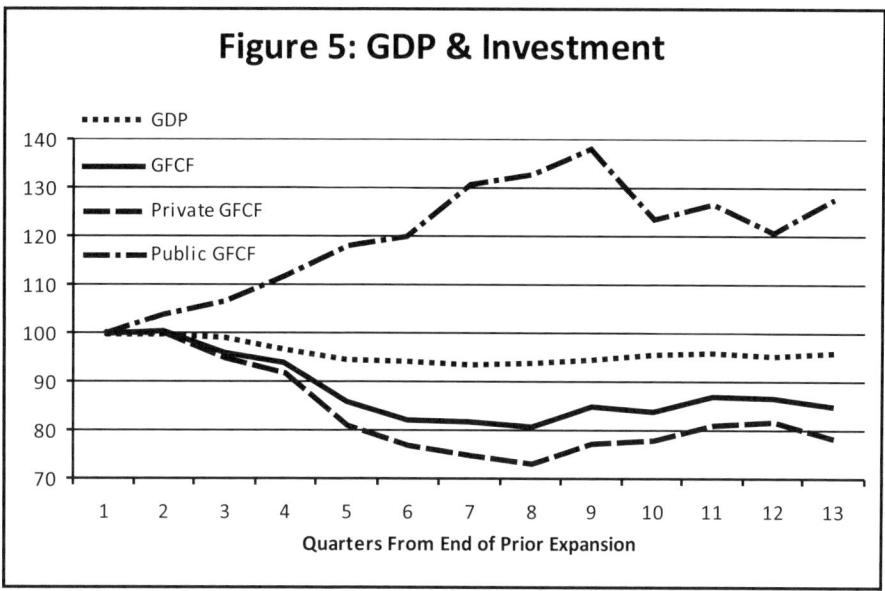

GDP and investment in the thirteen quarters since the end of the boom in the first quarter of 2008.

As already noted, the figures show that decline in investment is the driving force behind the recession and the subsequent failure to recover to the previous peak level of output. Private sector investment accounts for 79.8 per cent of that total shortfall in GDP. As Figure 5 shows, public investment moved in the opposite direction, increasing through 2008 and rising sharply in 2009, peaking in the first quarter of 2010 - the last quarter of the Labour government. By the time GDP began to recover modestly in the fourth quarter of 2009, public sector investment had risen by an annualised £10.5bn. This was far greater than the initial rise in GDP, which was just £6.1bn higher. Therefore the rise in public sector investment was entirely responsible for the recovery.

Private sector investment did not rise as soon as the economy began to expand. It began to rise only after recovery had begun. Since all private investment is determined by anticipated profits, this inability of the private sector to lead the recovery should be no surprise. However, over the course of 2010 private sector investment *was* the biggest single contributor to growth, rising by £22.3bn. This private sector investment increase was the result of growth that had been fostered by the sharp increase in the level of public sector investment. But instead of understanding that public sector investment was leading to economic recovery, including stimulating private sector investment, both the Tory-led government and the OBR subscribe to the idea that government spending 'crowds out' the private sector, so that if public spending is cut, private investment will increase. The opposite is in fact the case. Increased government investment 'crowds in' private investment.

The false Tory/OBR idea is further demonstrated by the negative reaction by the private sector to the subsequent cut in public sector investment. Public sector investment peaked in the first quarter of 2010, when it was 38.4 per cent higher than it was at the end of the prior business expansion. It began to fall as soon as the Tory-led Coalition took office in the second quarter of 2010. Shortly afterwards, in the fourth quarter of 2010, GDP began to stagnate. Immediately afterwards, private sector investment also began once more to contract. Clearly, the reason for the renewed decline in private sector investment - which accounts for 80 per cent of continued economic weakness - is the renewed weakness of the economy; and this is itself a function of the reduction in government spending.

An alternative policy

The problem of the private sector investment strike is a chronic one for the British economy, but it has recently become acute. The stagnation of the economy and the damage this is doing to Tory popularity has sparked a debate about the need for growth - led by Boris Johnson's call for tax cuts for those earning over £150,000 and for corporations.[2] But, predictably, this kind of response ignores that fact that the recovery was fostered by increased government spending, including investment, and is now being throttled by government spending cuts. The Tories' focus is on tax cuts for corporations and the rich, with many of them calling for an end to all carbon reduction policies, a reduction in the minimum wage, the abolition of employment laws, more privatisation, and so on.[3] This is a recipe for continued economic decline: as in other countries, such as Greece, Ireland and Portugal, the effect of such a huge transfer of incomes from poor to rich would be to depress economic activity even further, as well increasing the public sector deficit. Indeed, few of these ideas are likely to find much support outside Tory circles.

But one suggestion that has received some support is the idea of a corporate

Where did it all go wrong for George Osborne?

tax cut to boost investment. It is important to note, however, that this call ignores two important facts. First, the government is already cutting corporate tax rates from 28 per cent to 23 per cent, yet the private sector's investment strike is continuing, accounting for 80 per cent of total lost output. Secondly, the non-financial corporate sector is already sitting on a cash mountain of £695bn, which is simply financing dividend payments, enormous executive pay and takeovers - that is, everything but investment.[4]

The call for lower corporate taxes obscures a central truth about the current crisis. In any normally functioning market economy the household sector is a net saver. It retains a portion of its income and does not consume it immediately. These savings are mainly held in banks. The corporate sector is a normally a net borrower for investment, and borrows from the banks. The government can either be a saver (budget surplus) or borrower (budget deficit). This depends on its own tax and spending policies, but also on what happens in the rest of the economy. In the chart below, the level of lending or borrowing for these three main sectors is shown. Borrowing is a negative number and lending positive. Other important sectors (especially financial corporations and the rest of the world) have been disregarded for the sake of clarity. What the chart shows is that the British non-financial corporate sector has not been performing its designated role over a prolonged

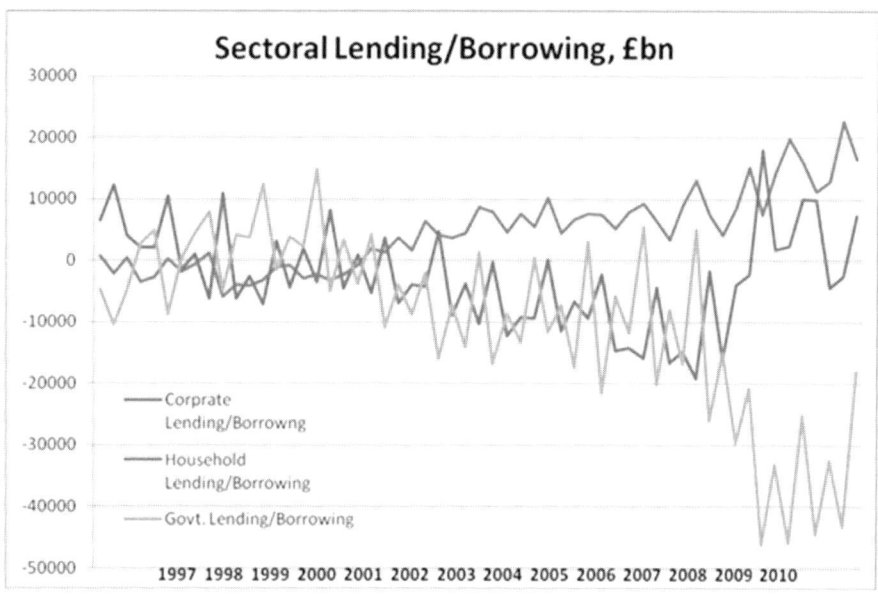

period. It has been a net saver. Disregarding the sectors not shown, in general the sum of these three sectors must balance to zero. Saving by one sector must have another sector its borrowing counterpart.

The saving of the corporate sector has had two effects. In the first instance corporate saving (achieved through lack of investment and low wages) has obliged the household sector to become a net borrower to finance consumption. It has also obliged the government to increase its borrowing as the lack of investment has depressed taxation revenues. When, at the beginning of 1998, the household sector took fright and returned rapidly to its traditional role of net saver, the government was obliged to sharply increase its own borrowing and the public sector deficit ballooned. The primary cause of both the unsustainable nature of the prior business expansion and the subsequent recession was the failure of the corporate sector to borrow to invest. Rather than cut their taxes and thus increase this saving, the whole thrust of policy should be designed to oblige the corporate sector to invest and to borrow for investment.

This highlights the essential failure of Labour to grasp the effects of its own policy proposals. Figure 2 above shows the planned fiscal tightening that was announced but never implemented in the March 2010 budget co-authored by Alistair Darling and Peter Mandelson. It shows that Labour would now be making a £26bn drain on the economy, in roughly the same proportion of tax increases and spending cuts that Osborne has implemented. Given that stagnation has been caused by just £9.4bn in cuts, the impact of a package nearly three times as great would evidently have been extremely damaging. But there has as yet been no clear break from this policy, and its accompanying mantra that Osborne is going 'too far, too fast' - though the call for a temporary cut in VAT and small boost to house building is a step in the right direction.[5]

It should by now be clear that it is not Osborne's speedometer that is faulty, but his navigation. His policy is diametrically opposite to that required. The corporate sector is saving, not investing. So, the failing policy prescription of cuts to the real incomes of households, via wage cuts, benefit cuts and public spending cuts, is entirely misdirected. It reduces the household sector's ability both to consume and to save. As a result, it increases the propensity to save of the corporate sector itself. Why would any business increase its investment when its two main customers, government and households, are both cutting back on their own spending?

Where did it all go wrong for George Osborne?

Instead, it is the policies of the 2009 Labour budget which can be seen to have worked: they produced an economic recovery and a falling public sector deficit. And this public-sector-led growth prompted a short-lived revival in private sector investment. But the improvement in public finances also appears to have stalled now, along with a stalled economy. However the revival of the economy and the reduction of the deficit are linked, the latter dependent on the former. Only an investment-led recovery can achieve sustainable growth and deficit-reduction. The corporate sector has demonstrated that it cannot lead that revival but will participate if it is sustained by public sector investment. Thus only increased government investment can currently lead economic recovery.

Michael Burke is an economic consultant who was previously senior international economist with Citibank in London.

Notes

1. IMF, 'Effects of stimulus in structural models': www.imf.org/external/pubs/ft/wp/2010/wp1073.pdf.

2. 'Boris Johnson tells George Osborne to cut National Insurance and 50p tax': www.telegraph.co.uk/news/politics/8664414/Boris-Johnson-tells-George-Osborne-to-cut-National-Insurance-and-50p-tax.html.

3. Conservativehome, 'Here you go George, a growth manifesto from London's think tanks', retrieved 26.7.11: http://conservativehome.blogs.com/thinktankcentral/2011/07/growthmanifesto.html.

4. ONS, UK Summary Accounts, Q1 2010, Table 9.1M (p156).

5. Ed Balls, speech to LSE, *New Statesman*, 16.6.11. www.newstatesman.com/politics/2011/06/george-osborne-growth-deficit.

'Cars not casinos': the manufacturing revival

Paul Everitt

Recent steps to rebalance the economy towards manufacturing are welcome, but need strengthening.

———

The UK motor industry is facing one of the most exciting and optimistic periods in its recent history. The recession and financial crisis have resulted in a fundamental reassessment of the value and importance of manufacturing. There is a huge growth in global demand for vehicles, mostly in the emerging BRIC economies, and there are significant shifts in technology as the industry transitions towards ultra-low carbon vehicles. These shifts place the UK motor industry at the heart of the drive to rebalance the economy towards manufacturing, creating valuable new jobs in the design, development and manufacture of low carbon products that we can export to markets around the world.

Such opportunities may come as a surprise to the many people that have written off the motor industry and manufacturing as something belonging to our industrial past, rather than our future. There have been huge changes in the industry during the last thirty years, and the sector has survived difficult economic cycles through sustained investment from global companies headquartered around the world. The attraction for global investors has included iconic British brands, a skilled and flexible workforce, excellent capability in key automotive technologies, an open and welcoming culture, and easy access to key markets. These attributes have helped to sustain the sector, but there has also been a significant shift in the political environment that has helped to re-position the industry and allowed it to play a

'Cars not casinos'

much bigger role in our economic future.

The sector is set to see output rise over the medium term, with a focus on higher value vehicles and delivering cleaner, safer and more fuel-efficient products. The following statistics give some indication of this:

- The UK is home to seven volume car manufacturers and nine commercial vehicle manufacturers.
- Nineteen of the world's top twenty component suppliers have operations in the UK.
- The UK was the fourth largest car producer in Europe in 2010 and had the third largest new car market.
- The UK produced almost 1.5 million vehicles in 2010 and 2.4 million engines.
- 75 to 80 per cent of production volume is for export markets.
- The automotive industry contributes to more than 10 per cent of total UK exports (by value).
- The automotive industry employs more than 700,000 people, with some 30 per cent in the manufacturing sector.
- More than £1.5 billion is spent annually on automotive R&D, with a strong emphasis on low carbon vehicles and manufacturing processes.

Vehicle production rose by 28 per cent in 2010 and engine output by 16 per cent, as the sector recovered following the recession. Vehicle and engine output has continued to rise in 2011, mainly on the back of exports, and further growth is expected in 2012 and 2013.

A key element in the robustness of the industry has been the positive relationships that have developed over the past decade between employees, trade unions and senior management teams, both nationally and internationally. These strong relationships are built upon a shared recognition that UK facilities are involved in intense competition for company investment. Management and employees understand that they will all lose if facilities in other parts of the world are seen to provide better investment opportunities. This mutual understanding binds employees and management in a set of shared goals. The strength of these relationships was demonstrated during the recession. Companies, employees and their trade union representatives worked together to find ways to accommodate the sudden reduction in demand. This meant all company employees accepting pay reductions and short-time working to ensure the minimum number of job losses. These actions have meant that as demand has returned UK facilities have been able to respond quickly and take advantage of favourable exchange rates and attractive model line-ups. The fundamental change in the relationships between companies and employees has been greatly aided by the social values most significant investors have brought to the UK motor industry. In Germany and Japan industrial practices and relationships place greater value on the contribution made by each employee, greater emphasis on the longer-term nature of the relationship and greater respect for the collaborative nature of the endeavour.

Changing attitudes to manufacturing

During the course of the last thirty to forty years the prevailing political orthodoxy was that the UK was a post-industrial economy, where future prosperity would be dependent on a dynamic service economy. But the financial crisis has led to a fundamental reassessment of our national interest, and of the importance of manufacturing as a generator of economic growth. Peter Mandelson, then Secretary of State for Business Innovation and Skills, made a speech in December 2008, which signalled a major change of emphasis.[1] In this key intervention he made a case for the concept of industrial activism, for the recognition of the strategic national importance of key sectors, and for the championing of specific measures to support industry during the crisis. This was widely regarded as a successful challenge to the Treasury's adherence to a free market philosophy.

It could, of course, be argued that the Labour government was late in recognising the value of a strong manufacturing sector. In countries across Europe and around the world many governments were already acting to limit the impact of the financial crisis on their domestic industrial capability. They were providing loans or loan guarantees to sustain supply chains, offering support to companies to retain employees, and looking at schemes to stimulate consumer demand. Nevertheless, the actions taken during Labour's last period in office were important in creating a new mood and laying the groundwork for important new investment.

'Cars not casinos'

Mandelson's speech outlined what he regarded as the five core principles of industrial activism. First, industrial activism does not mean propping up failed companies or running industries from Whitehall. Second, it means being pragmatic about the ability of markets to enable companies and people to succeed in a rapidly changing global economy. Third, industrial activism can't be reduced to industrial policy but needs to include regulation, planning policy, migration policy and transport policy, as well as the way government spends money and encourages innovation and entrepreneurship. Fourth, it means looking strategically at each sector in the economy in order to assess how horizontal policy can secure maximum benefits. Fifth, it means engaging in Europe and globally, to shape the institutions and policies that manage globalisation and global regulation, and make sure British companies are exploiting open markets.

In January 2009 Mandelson made a further speech in the House of Lords, in which he recognised the improvements that had taken place in the automotive industry and announced a support package to further strengthen it, commenting that: 'For the future, Britain needs an economy with less financial engineering and more real engineering. The car industry can and should be a vibrant part of that future'.[2] Ian Lucas, Parliamentary Under-Secretary at Mandelson's department from 2009-10, also played a role in securing support for the sector, in particular in his efforts to establish the UK Automotive Council, and in helping to create a different model of engagement with international businesses.

The policy and relationships established in the final period of the Labour government have been broadly taken forward by the Coalition government. Vince Cable and Mark Prisk have each endorsed the notion of a stronger role for manufacturing, a focus on low carbon and the need to engage with global investors. (Indeed in his 2011 party conference speech, Cable called for 'cars not casinos'.) The help and financial support promised to a number of vehicle manufacturers was delivered by the coalition. During the early days of the new government a range of initiatives were reviewed and then confirmed: the £5000 consumer incentive for ultra-low carbon vehicles; the infrastructure grant for electric vehicle charging; and a number of loan guarantees to help secure European Investment Bank loans. There is no doubt that the UK motor industry has benefited from this sense of continuity; an industrial agenda developed under one administration and taken forward by another has strengthened confidence across all businesses in the sector.

Soundings

It is worth noting, however, that this has not been the experience of all industries. The government's commitment to sustaining important industrial capability was not evident in its decision not to support Sheffield Forgemasters, its failure to award a rail contract to Bombardier in June 2011, and the impact on the defence sector of the strategic defence review. And some also argue that Mandelson's rhetoric on industrial activism did not deliver lasting change or fundamentally alter the free market ideology embedded within most politicians and officials.[3] But I believe his remarks were important, and helped the UK motor industry to convince international investors there were real opportunities here. There are important lessons for business and policy makers from the industry's experience.

The UK Automotive Council

In 2008 Richard Parry Jones, former Chief Technology Officer at Ford, was asked to produce a twenty-year vision for the future of the UK motor industry and make recommendations on how it could be achieved. A core team of senior people from across industry, the trade unions, government departments, regional development agencies and universities worked together to create a shared vision and a set of aspirations for the UK motor industry. They identified a number of factors that would be required for future success, including: a supportive government; industry co-ordination at a high level to facilitate greater non-competitive collaboration with a more coherent and effective interface with government; critical mass or scale for operations, supported by a progressive and strong home market able to showcase the next significant developments of the sector globally; availability of key skills - management, technical, manufacturing operations; and a capable, competitive, integrated supply chain.

The final report was submitted in early 2009, and it made clear that the industry faced significant short-term risks as a consequence of the scale and speed of the financial crisis, and the recession it had precipitated. Urgent action was required by government, to reassure global investors, and signal that they understood the longer-term challenges faced by the sector.

The UK government's response was to launch the Automotive Assistance Programme and the Scrappage Incentive Scheme, and to adapt the Train to Gain programme. The effectiveness of each of these initiatives has been questioned by

'Cars not casinos'

some, but together they sent a very clear and powerful signal to global vehicle manufacturers that the UK recognised the importance of the sector and would play its part in helping it sustain vital industrial capability during the exceptional circumstances that prevailed through 2009. The most important and effective response, however, was the establishment of a UK Automotive Council. This was joint industry/government body, co-chaired by the Secretary of State at the Department of Business and senior industry leaders, whose aim was to transform the business environment for the automotive industry and create a more compelling investment proposition for national and international companies. Its main streams of activity are around low carbon technology, strengthening the supply chain and more effective communication.

The UK Automotive Council has recognised the importance of being at the forefront of the shift to ultra-low carbon vehicles. Regulation in key markets around the world will require manufacturers to deliver progressively low, lower and ultra-low carbon vehicles, and this means that the environmental necessity for change is also an industrial opportunity. The Council has therefore developed a low carbon technology roadmap, supported by an analysis of UK technology capability. These studies provided the basis for industry to identify a set of priority technologies that were crucial to delivering a low carbon future, and to identify where the UK had a competitive advantage in contributing to this. The technologies identified were next-generation combustion engines, energy storage, lightweight materials and structures, and advanced electronics. These priorities are now being used to guide collaborative R&D projects and programmes, with funding from the Technology Strategy Board, government departments and the Research Councils.

The Council also recognises the big opportunity that exists for a strengthened and thriving UK supply base (though there has been a steady erosion of supply capability during the last forty years and reversing this will take time). Working with vehicle manufacturers and suppliers, the Council has developed a sourcing roadmap that highlights the key commodities and technologies that vehicle manufacturers want to buy in the UK. It has found that a high proportion of industry needs can be met from UK based suppliers, and that there is a real appetite from vehicle manufacturers to secure increased UK sourcing. A number of factors underpin this shift in outlook, one of which is that the cost savings many hoped to achieve in moving their sourcing to eastern Europe and Asia have not materialised, as a consequence of increasing transport costs, rapid wage inflation, instability in extended supply chains and concerns about quality. All this meant that companies had to hold greater quantities of stock, which undermined the just-in-time production processes most operate. The Council is now helping to facilitate relationships between manufacturers and potential suppliers, and will be running a series of focused events to identify suppliers from other sectors - such as aerospace and motorsport - which may have skills or technologies in demand across the motor industry.

The third stream of work being undertaken by the Council seeks to improve the image of UK manufacturing, in the context of a widespread concern that the UK's reputation as a leading high-value manufacturer is poorly understood. It has been co-ordinating a campaign to build a better understanding of modern manufacturing among students, careers advisers and parents. This is particularly important given that the perception of many parents and teachers was formed in the 1970s and 1980s, when manufacturing was in decline and offered few job opportunities. Its 'See Inside Manufacturing' initiative aims to give young people and those that influence them the opportunity to see for themselves what happens in manufacturing. Under this scheme, UK motor industry facilities for the design, development, manufacture and testing of vehicles are being opened up to show the types of jobs and working conditions that exist.

The Council is also focusing its attention on the international business leaders who determine the investment decisions of global vehicle manufacturers and component suppliers. It is extremely important that these executives understand that the UK appreciates their investment and wants to work with them to secure further opportunities. Direct engagement with these business leaders is important in convincing them that the commitments made to a rebalanced economy, and the priorities to be given to manufacturing, are real and will be long-term. The UK Automotive Council is now working closely with UK Trade & Investment to better co-ordinate activities and to target those with genuine interest and opportunity to invest in Britain.

What next?

In the motor industry there is now a reasonably well defined strategy for securing future growth, and the challenge for business and government now is to deliver it.

'Cars not casinos'

The industry is well placed, but there is no room for complacency. Economies in every corner of the globe are seeking to attract highly mobile investment, and British manufacturers must be prepared to compete vigorously for their share.

One area of growing concern concerns the strength of demand in the UK domestic economy. The impact of tax increases, public expenditure cuts and the cost of living squeeze has meant a low and slow-paced recovery. So far the manufacturing sector, buoyed by strong export demand, has had some success as a driving force within the economy. If this is to be sustained, a step-change increase in the level of investment in R&D, skills and capital equipment must be engineered.

Investment in R&D adds significant value to the economy. It encourages relationships between global companies and specialist technology providers, thereby embedding industrial capability in the UK supply chain and attracting new investors. The competitive R&D funding provided by the Technology Strategy Board has so far proved extremely effective. An overall increase in its funding would send a strong positive signal to businesses about the UK's commitment to high value research. It is also important that collaborative R&D is focused in the areas of most interest to companies. Government should work with the Technology Strategy Board and industry to identify major projects or programmes that would help equip UK industry for the future. It is likely that the low carbon challenge faced by the automotive industry will be replicated across a number of sectors, and it therefore justifies significant additional public investment. Furthermore, the Treasury can help to make R&D undertaken in the UK more attractive. The current R&D tax credit system could work better for larger companies by increasing the rate and allowing it to be offset against other UK taxes. This would give the tax credit system more visibility when major R&D decisions are being taken, and would help to reduce the headline cost of undertaking work in Britain.

A closer working relationship between UK research councils, universities and industry would help to ensure that more resources were focused into areas where there are future commercial opportunities. This could generate a strong pipeline of good ideas and technology to important industrial sectors and help equip students with the knowledge and experience that is most likely to be in demand. Skills also remain an issue of great importance. The resurgence of interest in manufacturing will be threatened if there is a failure to adequately address skills and training. There are three areas of challenge: attracting young people into the industry and equipping them appropriately; making sure those already employed have the opportunity to regularly refresh and improve their skills; and providing a route into regular employment for those that may have missed out on structured training first time round.

Skills and training have been given a degree of priority by successive governments, and there are excellent people and schemes working in this area. But many companies and employees find the skills landscape cluttered and confusing. The wide variety of different funding bodies, support organisations, scheme criteria and mechanisms dissuades all but the most determined. Larger companies with dedicated resources are able to navigate the system, but it can still feel unnecessarily slow and bureaucratic. Simplifying the system and giving greater control to those creating the demand for training is very important. Large companies must also play a central role in meeting skills challenges: with the right incentives they could be encouraged to systematically train more apprentices than the firm required. This would mean a steady stream of qualified people being made available to smaller companies in the supply chain. Similarly, larger companies could be encouraged to work with their suppliers to help upskill their workforce.

Maintaining workforce flexibility as UK advantage is also extremely important. The cyclical nature of demand in the motor industry and other manufacturing sectors makes the use of agency workers an important part of the UK's industrial proposition. But there should be scope for closer collaboration between employers, trade unions and government to help support employees that find themselves out of work. A recently launched initiative aims to help link up companies with vacancies and people who are, or are about to be, looking for work. The scheme is designed to maintain the base of manufacturing skills and prevent skilled workers leaving the sector. It recognises that at a regional level there will be a variety of manufacturing businesses operating in different sectors with different cycles of demand. So, for example, if companies in the aerospace and automotive manufacturers in the Derby area are seeing demand grow they might be able to help offset job losses being seen in the rail sector. If this basic concept, already endorsed and actively supported by trades unions, could be supplemented with additional training, careers advice and help with travel or relocation costs, it would add value to the whole industry. Employers would be confident of finding appropriately skilled staff, and individuals would have the reassurance of an established infrastructure to manage any short-term breaks in their employment.

The UK will always be a high-cost country, and we must compete by being more productive and innovative than our competitors. This requires sustained investment in new plant, machinery and processes. The Treasury can help in this by ensuring the tax regime incentivises investment in the real economy through capital allowances and annual investment allowances. There is also an opportunity for government - national and local - to review the business rate systems for manufacturing facilities. Some relatively minor changes in the way factories are assessed for rateable value would increase their attractiveness for new investment. A small reduction in business rate income could easily be offset by the additional revenue generated by higher employment and economic activity.

To succeed companies need to invest, and this requires a financial community that is prepared to offer appropriate loans and capital support. Despite the positive growth in UK vehicle and engine production, new investment by vehicle manufacturers, and clearly articulated desire to increase the level of UK sourcing, too many companies struggle to find affordable finance. This must change. Banks and their shareholders need to begin to value the long-term returns that successful manufacturing businesses generate. The culture of short-termism, so damagingly revealed during the financial crisis, has to change. The financial sector must see itself as part of the broader business community, with a responsibility to help encourage and foster successful enterprise. The structural reforms currently being considered by the Independent Commission on Banking are likely to be insufficient to address the short-termism prevalent in many financial institutions. Greater transparency on the risks of investments and the rewards to senior executives may do more to encourage shareholders to take a more active interest in governance issues.

Finally

The UK has the potential to become a leading twenty-first century manufacturing nation. Despite the impact of a series of recessions and the ambivalence of successive governments, it retains important technology capabilities, a flexible and highly regarded workforce, and an industrial infrastructure that allows it to be globally competitive across a number of important sectors.

The choices Britain now makes, and its willingness to challenge the behaviours and accepted constraints of recent decades, will shape the opportunities on offer to current and future generations. The impact of the financial crisis and the need for fiscal consolidation requires the private sector to take the lead in generating jobs and prosperity. The government must use its limited resources to encourage and incentivise investment in the broader social goods represented by research and development, skills and new plant and machinery.

The regeneration of UK manufacturing is essential for our economic well being. Its success will create many thousands of good jobs, providing a sense of direction, structure and hope for many of those who have been left behind or disenchanted by the years of boom and bust. Those working in the UK motor industry and broader manufacturing retain a sense of pride and self-esteem from the work they do. Producing real things that are useful, have value and are in demand, is a social and economic opportunity for the UK. The challenge for policy-makers is to prioritise the needs of manufacturing - supporting investment for the long-term and equipping people with the skills they need to succeed in a tough and globally competitive world.

Paul Everitt joined the Society of Motor Manufacturers and Traders in January 2008 as Chief Executive. He was a member of the New Automotive Innovation and Growth Team and is now a member of the Automotive Council. He has been a leading advocate for the strategic importance of the UK motor industry. He was previously Director of Civil Air Transport and Communications at the Society of British Aerospace Companies.

Notes

1. Mandelson's speech to the RSA on 'a new industrial activism', December 2008: http://webarchive.nationalarchives.gov.uk/+/http://www.berr.gov.uk/aboutus/ministerialteam/Speeches/page49416.html

'Cars not casinos'

2. Mandelson's speech in House of Lords announcing automotive support package, January 2009: http://news.bbc.co.uk/1/hi/uk_politics/7854329.stm

3. For one critique of this speech see Howard Reed's review of it in *Soundings* 44: www.lwbooks.co.uk/journals/soundings/archive/review44.html.

The entrepreneurial state

Mariana Mazzucato

Overlooking the key role of the state in promoting innovation is one of the biggest mistakes of market fundamentalism.

The current debate, in the UK and abroad, on the need to cut back the state in order to unleash the power of entrepreneurship and innovation in the private sector, builds upon a stark contrast that is repeatedly drawn by the media, business and libertarian politicians: a dynamic, creative competitive private sector versus a sluggish, bureaucratic, inert, 'meddling' public sector. Company heads complain about the state stifling innovation; in the US, Tea Party politicians call for the state not to meddle in areas like healthcare that are more efficiently run by the market; David Cameron calls civil sector workers the 'enemies of enterprise', and editorials in the *Economist* call for the public sector to be reduced to open up opportunities for innovation and competition.

In painting this contrast, it is assumed that the private sector is inherently more innovative, more able to think out of the 'box' and to lead a country towards long-run innovation-led growth. In this view, the retrenchment of the public sector will inherently make the economy more productive and achieve higher growth. But many examples in the history of innovation, entrepreneurship and competition, in different sectors and across different countries, paint a very different picture - of a risk taking innovative state - especially in the most uncertain phases of technological development and/or in the most risky sectors - versus a more inert private sector, which only invests (in innovation, in new start-ups, in networks) once the state has absorbed most of the uncertainty.

There are plenty of examples. In the pharmaceutical industry it is the state-run labs that have been responsible for the discovery of the most radical new important drugs, with private pharma focused on the less risky slight variations of existing, 'me too', drugs (such as Viagra in different colours and dosages). In the USA and Europe, state funding has been responsible for most, if not all, general purpose technologies, i.e. those technologies that help achieve economy-wide growth (aviation, computers, electricity, internet, nanotechnology). The biotech revolution owes its success not to venture capital (as is commonly assumed) but to major inventions within the UK's Medical Research Council and the US's National Institute of Health, as well as pro-innovation regulations that have made it easier for these inventions to be commercialised. This has not been just a question of 'research', but of the state having the courage to think about completely new areas of development, invest its resources into uncertain territory, open multiple windows of exploration, fund early-stage risky research, create organisations dedicated to funding and supporting new start-ups, and formulate dynamic 'networks' between science, business and finance.

In most cases of the development of general purpose technology it has been the state that has gone against the grain, thought 'out of the box', risked large amounts of money; while the private sector has more often been wedded to the status quo, where short-run returns are inevitably more secure. Similar examples can be found in the creative sector, where, for example, innovative first-time directors can 'enter' the industry only through risky state-backed funds or state-owned broadcasters. In this sense, the state has played a role that goes beyond the Keynesian emphasis on taxation, subsidies, spending and regulation, and the Schumpeterian emphasis on creating the 'right conditions' for innovation and growth. It has played an active entrepreneurial role - envisioning new technological opportunities in high-growth areas; undertaking the very early risky investments that lay the groundwork for future exploration of these areas; funding new start-ups that commercialize the innovations; and in some cases even bringing the product to market. It has in fact not only solved 'market failure' (of which there are many instances); more importantly, it has solved 'network' or 'opportunity' failures. It has not only 'fixed' markets; it has actively led the creation of new ones.

The entrepreneurial state

Beyond market failures

The view of the current UK government regarding its role in stimulating innovation is to create an environment where the private sector can flourish. Indeed, a recent growth review by the Department for Business, Innovation and Skills and HM Treasury stated that its role is to 'provide the conditions for private sector growth and investment'.[1] This is the view that sees government as having a role only for the purpose of correcting market failures - for example through investment in basic science, education and infrastructure. The arguments in favour of limiting the role of the state and relying on the market for innovation are not new, but they would benefit from a greater understanding of the academic literature on the role of innovation in creating economic growth.

Entrepreneurship, like growth, is one of the least understood topics in economics. Entrepreneurship involves taking risk.[2] It is not just a question of setting up a new business (the more common definition), but of doing so in a way that produces a new product, or a new process, or a new market for an existing product or process. According to Schumpeter, regarded by some as a key theorist of entrepreneurialism, an entrepreneur is a person, or group of people, who is willing and able to convert a new idea or invention into a successful innovation. Entrepreneurship employs 'the gale of creative destruction' to replace inferior innovations across markets and industries, simultaneously creating new products, including new business models, and in so doing destroying the lead of the incumbents.[3] In this way, creative destruction is largely responsible for the dynamism of industries and long-run economic growth. Each major new technology leads to creative destruction: the steam engine, the railway, electricity, electronics, the car, the computer, the internet have all destroyed as much as they have created, but have also led to increased wealth overall.

In fact, entrepreneurial risk-taking, like technological change, is not just risky; it is highly 'uncertain'. Frank Knight distinguished risk from uncertainty in the following way:

> The practical difference between the two categories, risk and uncertainty, is that in the former the distribution of the outcome in a group of instances is known ... While in the case of uncertainty

that is not true, the reason being in general that it is impossible to form a group of instances, because the situation dealt with is in a high degree unique.[4]

Technological change is a good example of the truly unique situation, since not only do R&D investments take years to materialise into new products, but most investments lead to failure. In the pharmaceutical sector, for example, innovation takes up to seventeen years from the beginning of an R&D project to the end. It costs about $403 million per drug and the failure rate is extremely high. Only one in 10,000 compounds reaches market approval phase - a success rate of 0.01 per cent. When successful, the search for one product often leads to the discovery of a completely different one. The process is characterised by serendipity.[5] This of course does not mean that innovation is based on luck. Far from it. It is based on long-term strategies and targeted investments. But the returns from those investments are highly uncertain and thus cannot be understood through rational economic theory (this is one of the critiques that modern-day Schumpeterians make of endogenous growth theory, which models R&D as a game-theoretic choice).

The high risk and serendipitous nature of the innovation process is one of the main reasons why profit-maximising companies invest less in basic research and more in applied research - there are greater and more immediate returns from the latter. Investment in basic research is a typical example of 'market failure': the market alone does not produce enough basic research, which means that government must step in. This is why there are few people, on all sides of the political spectrum, who would disagree that it should be (and is) the state that in general funds most basic research. In the US economy, for example, while government spending on R&D makes up only 26 per cent of total R&D, with the private sector making up 67 per cent, the proportion is much higher when basic research is considered in isolation. Indeed public spending accounts for 57 per cent of basic research in the USA, with the private sector taking on only 18 per cent.

The concept of market failure is inadequate as a way of understanding the role of government in the innovation process because it ignores a fundamental fact about the history of innovation. Not only has government funded the most risky research, whether applied or basic, but it has also frequently been the source of the most radical, path-breaking types of innovation. To this extent it has actively created markets, rather than simply fixing them.

Large-scale and long-term government investment has been the engine behind almost every general purpose technology. In analysing the development of six different technology complexes (the US 'mass production' system, aviation technologies, space technologies, information technology, internet technologies and nuclear power), Ruttan reached the conclusion that government investments have been of some importance in bringing these new technologies into being - and that nuclear power would probably not have been developed at all without large government investments in development.[6] In each case he looked at, support for the development of technology involved not only the funding of innovation and creating the right conditions, but also the envisioning of opportunity space, an engagement in the most risky and uncertain early research, and the overseeing of the commercialisation process. This is also the case for the current development of nanotechnology, which many believe is the next general purpose technology.

At a more micro level, Fred Block and Matthew Keller found that between 1971 and 2006, seventy-seven out of the most important eighty-eight innovations in the USA (rated by *R&D Magazine*'s annual awards) were found to have been fully dependent on federal support, especially, but not only, in the early phases.[7]

Across a number of different sectors, it has often been the state that has funded the most radical innovations, while the private sector has focused on the less risky, more profitable innovations. Venture capital itself has often entered the field too late (when the core risk has been absorbed by the state sector), and with the sole interest of making a buck from the initial public offering process, rather than of following through to make sure that the companies it invests in actually produce anything (for example the majority of venture capital backed biotech companies remain product-less[8]).

Ironically, the state has played this innovatory role most strongly in the USA, which is usually described in European policy circles and in the media as one in which the economy is mainly driven by the market, with many European politicians pitching the need to learn from the market-driven Silicon Valley experiment. Silicon Valley was in fact built upon decades of state-led vision about the power of the internet, decades of investment in the riskiest research, and decades of nurturing regional innovation systems and new company start-ups - a lesson that is, ironically, now being ignored by the UK but followed by China. Block and Keller describe how, because of political pressure, the state's work in this area has operated in a 'hidden' way, through a decentralised network of state agencies such as the Defense Advanced Research Projects Agency and Small Business Innovation Research.[9]

Lessons for green technologies

In the pages of the *Economist* it was recently claimed that the 'government has a terrible record at picking winners' (28.4.11) - and this was applied to *all* governments, as an economic entity. But a look at the massive impact of the state's targeted large investments in industries such as steel, railroads, air travel, silicon microchip manufacturing, automotive manufacturing, computers, biotechnology, the internet and nanotechnology shows that this is simply untrue. Without the government pursuing a targeted investment strategy, none of these industries would have come into being.

Today there is a global race to be the leader in green technologies. Britain has a potential to do well in this race, but is in danger of being left behind if it adheres to this myth about the state's limited role in economic policy. Innovation policy needs to focus on creating the conditions that allow innovation to flourish, but also, and perhaps especially, on directly commissioning and procuring innovative solutions. History tells us that these will not happen without a strong push by the state.

In the USA's stimulus packages, 11.5 per cent of the budget was for green investment, while in the UK the figure is only 6.9 per cent, far lower than China (34.3 per cent), France (21 per cent) or South Korea (80.5 per cent).[10] In fact, in July 2010 the South Korean government announced that it would double its spending on green research to the equivalent of £1.9 billion by 2013 (almost 2 per cent of its annual GDP), which means that between 2009 and 2013 it will have spent £59 billion on this type of research.

This lack of public investment is not a new problem. Data for 2007 shows the UK near the bottom of the league when comparing government investment in energy R&D, spending less than US and Asian competitors and some other

The entrepreneurial state

European countries. The problem is that, contrary to the prevailing orthodoxy, the private sector is not coming in to fill the gap. This means that, overall, the UK's investment of 12.6 billion in 2009-2010 is less than 1 per cent of GDP - half of what South Korea currently invests in green technologies annually, and less than the UK presently spends on furniture in a year.[11]

Lessons from previous developments of major technologies teach us that innovation is about having the right networks in the economy and then commissioning specific technologies; and it could be argued that scaling back direct subsidies and grants, regardless of the purpose, would not be troublesome as long as innovative forces were coming from elsewhere. However, a look at recent data seems to imply that this is not the case. In fact, the UK is at risk of falling behind in this area, in spite of having been seen as a country that was catching up in the last decade.

Since green technology is still in its very early stage, when Knightian uncertainty is highest, capital funding - as might be expected - is focused on some of the safer bets, rather than on the radical innovation that is so needed if the sector is to reach the 20-20-20 targets.[12] This is highly problematic since the early stage of development of the sector means that by definition many of the needed developments are both risky and capital intensive; this means that if the government does not make its mark, these important areas will remain underdeveloped. Venture capitalists are increasingly targeting incremental innovations in established technologies to improve energy efficiency, moving away from more radical forms of innovation for energy production. And these preferences for familiar technology and quick payback add to fears that a renewed 'dash for gas' may turn out to be the most likely route for the UK to try to meet its emissions reduction commitments, even though this will add to the dangers of energy insecurity and of sharply rising costs when gas reserves begin to deplete.

The conclusion that might follow from this lack of private investment is that the government needs to be commissioning the development of the riskiest technologies. But this is not happening. The main initiative of the Coalition government is to establish a green investment bank to provide seedcorn funding for green technologies. In accordance with its general approach, this is based on the notion that the green revolution can be led privately, simply 'incentivised' by the state. This is wrong (no other tech revolution has occurred this way); and the current amounts being discussed are in any case too insignificant to make any difference. The green investment bank initiative has not learned from previous revolutions that have shown the importance of active state-led investments, which have allowed these states to 'be first' and hence reap future increasing returns. China is building one power station a week and Britain is fiddling with play money.

Improving the UK's aging energy infrastructure will require massive investments. The proposed green investment bank could help to get important projects off the drawing board. However, as the cash for it is dependent on selling off strategic assets in difficult market conditions, it will take many months or even years before the fund is able to make a meaningful difference. And the current figures are of negligible significance. However, if it was expanded and broadened, the green investment bank could grow into a strategic investment bank, like the European Investment Bank or Germany's Kreditanstalt fur Wiederaufbau. These have a proven track record of promoting infrastructure development and returning a profit for the taxpayer; while the UK has always lacked a comparable source of long-term finance, and would gain from developing one. If such a government-run investment bank took more of an innovation focus than the European Investment Bank and Kreditanstalt fur Wiederaufbau, it could become a new type of public-sector strategic finance institution. This would be particularly helpful in getting large-scale projects off the ground. But even so, it would not necessarily be capable of providing the incentive for the high risk innovative breakthroughs to occur in the first place.

Risk and return: smart and inclusive growth

In finance, it is commonly accepted that there is a relationship between risk and return. However, in the innovation game this has not been the case. Risk taking has been a collective endeavour, while the returns have been much less collectively distributed. The only return that the state usually gets for its risky investments are the indirect benefits of higher tax receipts that result from the growth that is generated by those investments. Is that enough?

There is indeed lots of talk of partnership between the government and private

The entrepreneurial state

sector, but while the efforts are collective, the returns remain private. Is it right that the National Science Foundation did not reap any financial return from funding the grant that produced the algorithm that led to Google's search engine? Can an innovation system based on government support be sustainable with such a system of rewards? The lack of knowledge in the public domain about the central entrepreneurial role that government plays in the growth of economies worldwide is currently putting a successful model in major danger.

The socialised generation but privatised commercialisation of biopharmaceutical - and other - technologies could be followed by withdrawal of the state, if private companies were to use their profits to reinvest in research and further product development. The state's role would then be limited to that of initially underwriting radical new discoveries, until they are generating profits that can fund on-going discovery. But private-sector behaviour suggests that public institutions cannot pass on the R&D baton in this way. This means that the state's role cannot be limited to that of planting seeds that can be subsequently relied on to grow without further intervention.

A fairer and more dynamic relationship between risk and return requires a more informed understanding of the state's leading role in taking on risk. When SITRA, the Finnish government's public innovation fund, provided the early stage funding for Nokia, it later reaped a significant return on this investment - a fact accepted by the Finnish business community and politicians. The reason why the US government has not reaped a return from its early stage investments in companies like Google (which benefitted from a state-funded grant for its early algorithm), and other such success stories, including Apple and Compaq (which both received public funding), is due to the lack of understanding in the USA of state-led growth-inducing investments. And this allows conservative forces to portray the state as only ever a menace in the economy. But as governments all over the world are fighting hard to put their finances in order, while simultaneously needing to find the funds and opportunities to make necessary growth-inducing investments (in education, research, infrastructure, etc), finding ways to reap a return from such investments is more important than ever. Such returns could help provide funds that can be re-plugged back into the economy, helping to assure a virtuous cycle, rather than the current vicious one.

Conclusion

The state has been fundamentally involved in generating radically new products and processes that have changed the way that businesses operate and citizens live - transforming economies forever, from the internet revolution to the biotech revolution to what (it is hoped) will be the green-tech revolution. A key way to tackle together smart and inclusive growth is to ensure that the gains from innovation are as collective as the risk-taking underlying it.

In seeking innovation-led growth, it is fundamental to understand the important roles that both the public and private sector can play. This requires not only understanding the different ecologies between the public and private sector, but, especially, rethinking what it is that the public is bringing to that ecology. The claim that the public sector can at best incentivise private sector led innovation (through subsidies, tax reductions, carbon pricing, green investment banks and so on) is currently being propagated heavily in the UK, especially but not only in the face of the recent crisis and ensuing deficits. But this fails to account for the many examples in which the leading entrepreneurial force came from the state rather than from the private sector.

Mariana Mazzucato is RM Professor of Science and Technology Policy at the University of Sussex, and Professor in the Economics of Innovation at the Open University. She is Economics Director of the ESRC Centre for Socio-Economic Study of the Genomics (INNOGEN www.genomicsnetwork.ac.uk/innogen/) and Coordinator of a European Commission FP7 funded project on Finance, Innovation and Growth (FINNOV www.finnov-fp7.eu). Her most recent publication is *The Entrepreneurial State*, Demos 2011: www.demos.co.uk/publications/theentrepreneurialstate.

Notes

1. Department for Business, Innovation and Skills and HM Treasury, *The Plan for Growth*, March 2011, http://cdn.hm-treasury.gov.uk/2011budget_growth.pdf.

The entrepreneurial state

2. F. Knight, *Risk, Uncertainty and Profit*, Augustus M. Kelley, 1921; P. Drucker, *Technology, Management and Society*, Butterworth-Heinemann 1970.

3. J. Schumpeter, *Capitalism, Socialism and Democracy*, Harper, 1975 [1942]; and 'Economic theory and entrepreneurial history' [1949], in R. Clemence (ed), *Essays on Entrepreneurs, Innovations, Business Cycles, and the Evolution of Capitalism*, Transaction Publishers 1989.

4. *Risk, Uncertainty and Profit*.

5. In numerous historical instances scientific theory and explanations have emerged after the technologies they are seeking to explain. For example the Wright brothers flew before aerodynamics was developed, and the steam engine was operational before thermodynamics was understood.

6. V. Ruttan, *Is War Necessary for Economic Growth?: Military procurement and technology development*, Oxford University Press 2006.

7. F. Block and M. Keller, 'Where do innovations come from?' in F. Block and M. Keller (eds), *State of Innovation: The US government's role in technology development*, Paradigm, 2010.

8. W. Lazonick and O. Tulum, 'US biopharmaceutical finance and the sustainability of the biotech business model', *Research Policy 2011* (forthcoming).

9. A full account of this story, and its implications for understanding the economics of growth and innovation, can be found in my recent pamphlet, *The Enterpreneurial State*, Demos 2011.

10. PIRC, *The Green Investment Gap: An audit of green investment in the UK*, Public Interest Research Centre, March 2011.

11. *The Green Investment Gap*. The figure of £12.6 billion of UK green investment in 2009-10 was made up of total public investment to the amount of £6.7 billion (public subsidy, government loans and levies) and total private investment to the amount of £5.9 billion (asset finance, public markets, venture capital and private equity).

12. See S. Ghosh and R. Nanda, 'Venture capital investment in the cleantech sector', *Harvard Business School Working Paper* 11-020, 2010. The 20-20-20

strategy seeks a 20 per cent cut in emissions of greenhouse gases between 1990 to 2020, as well as a 20 per cent increase in the share of renewables in the energy mix, and a 20 per cent cut in energy consumption. See European Commission Climate Action, 'The EU climate and energy package', http://ec.europa.eu/clima/policies/package/index_en.htm).

Online access to Marx and Gramsci

You can now read online the complete works of Marx and Engels and all Gramsci works published by L&W – made possible through our partnership with Electric Book (http://www.elecbook.com/).

The texts are available through a pay as you go system. Starting with an initial payment of as little as £5, you can browse and download pages until your credit runs out (Marx and Gramsci pages are charged at 3p a page). Once a page has been viewed and paid for, you can read it as many times as you like without paying anything more. There are no subscription charges and no obligation to continue.

Electric Book comes with a very sophisticated search engine which allows full text search as well as proximity, Boolean, fuzzy and phonic searches, and searches on metadata like title, author or subject. Search an individual title or across the entire collection in less than a second. You can also bookmark any page and add notes, as well as create your own bookshelf for your chosen titles.

To find out more, go to http://www.elecbook.com/

Note: Electric Book has a large number of titles for other publishers on the site and will be adding more in the near future.

'Managed' v 'market capitalism': the record

Stewart Lansley

On almost every measure, the managed capitalism of the postwar era beats its 'free-market' successor

---

From the early 1980s, the British economy became the subject of an all-embracing economic experiment. At the heart of this economic leap-in-the-dark was a switch in philosophy from the 'managed capitalism' of the post-war era to one of 'market capitalism'. The former commitments to full employment, progressive taxation and inclusive welfare were dropped. Most elements of the post-war settlement - and its belief in economic fine-tuning, greater equality and a strong state - were discarded. Regulations were swept away and corporate and top income tax rates axed. Markets were given more freedom. Although this shift to market capitalism was applied most strongly in the United Kingdom and the United States, weaker versions were eventually introduced across much of the rich world.

The experiment came with big promises. The medicine of the market, it was claimed, would overturn the failings of post-war welfare capitalism. The 'supply-side' measures - weakening the power of collective bargaining, reducing taxes at the top and giving business and finance more freedom - would unleash a new era of enterprise, entrepreneurialism and dynamism. The elevation of finance to a more central place in the economy would lower financial risk. Freeing up markets would raise Britain's growth rate, create more jobs and businesses and bring greater prosperity for all. Countries like the United States and the UK which adopted extensive deregulation would experience less economic turbulence.

The new theories on the virtues of freer markets were developed from the 1960s,

'Managed' v 'market capitalism': the record

mainly by a group of American economists, from Milton Friedman to Robert Lucas, many of whom were based or had trained at the University of Chicago. Central to the new philosophy was a belief in efficient and self-regulating markets. Using the tools of advanced mathematics, these prophets of the market school constructed highly sophisticated and rigorously tested economic models that claimed to demonstrate that free and flexible financial and labour markets deliver greatly superior economic outcomes - on employment, productivity and growth - than regulated ones, and that government failure was much more likely than market failure. They also welcomed the personal wealth booms that accompanied the birth of the free-market era. Greater inequality was interpreted as a healthy sign that markets were working. According to their economic models, markets were self-regulating, economic shocks would quickly be reversed, while any tendency to imbalance would be quickly corrected provided markets were free to adjust.

So what about the record of the thirty-year long era of market economics? Has the market experiment delivered on its claims? Have Britain and the other countries adopting the market model, such as the United States, enjoyed greater economic prosperity and stability than in the more interventionist post-war era?

For a decade from the mid-to-late 1990s, it seemed that the new prophets might be right. After serious birth pangs in the 1980s and early 1990s - when restrictive macroeconomic policies blunted growth rates - the more open and globalised world economy entered a period of sustained growth. Although this upward path faltered slightly in 2000 and 2001 with the bursting of the new economy bubble, average growth rates across the world and the richer nations were higher between 1997 and 2007 than they had been in the period 1981-1996. Growth in both the UK and the US - an annual average of 3.0 and 3.3 per cent respectively in the decade to 2007 - outstripped that of the other G7 nations less wedded to markets (Japan, Germany, France, Italy and Canada), which averaged between them only 2.4 per cent.[1] These figures lent some support to the market school.

But we now know that this apparently promising economic performance, a solid improvement compared with the 1980s and early 1990s, was an illusion. One study, by the City brokerage firm Tullett Prebon has estimated that, after stripping out what they call 'the Brown bubble borrowing', the UK's real growth from 2000 to 2008 was half its headline rate. Half the much vaunted growth over this period was artificial. Moreover, while the contribution to the economy made by financial services (the 'bubble effect') more than doubled over this period, manufacturing shrank by a quarter and mining by more than a quarter. During the UK's post-millennium boom years, the money and productive sectors of the economy were moving in opposite directions.[2]

There was no economic miracle. Freer markets, and the escalating rewards at the top to which they gave rise, failed to deliver the sustained improvement in economic performance that had been promised. For their advocates, the new economic orthodoxy was to be judged above all on its impact on the real economy, on whether it delivered more productive, efficient and innovative economies. Yet the evidence is that market capitalism has been weaker on most key measures of economic performance than the period of managed capitalism. This is clear from dividing the post-war era into two distinct periods. The first - the 23-year period of 'managed capitalism' - dates from 1950 to 1973, the year of the first OPEC oil shock and the one which perhaps best marks the end of the post-war boom. The second period - the 29 years of 'market capitalism' - covers the period from 1980 to 2009, beginning with the first full year of the new economic experiment.[3]

Of course, there was no shortage of problems facing the UK economy in the 1950s and 1960s, from periodic sterling crises and an outdated industrial structure to falling competitiveness and deteriorating industrial relations. But, on only one count - curbing inflation - can the post-1980 era be judged a clear success. Inflation rates tailed off during the 1980s and have remained lower ever since. On all other counts, the economic record of market capitalism has been inferior to that of managed capitalism. Growth and productivity rates have been slower, and unemployment levels higher. As the proceeds of growth have been very unequally divided, the wealth gap has soared, without the promised pay-off of wider economic progress. Financial crises have become more frequent and more damaging in their consequences.

The record on growth and unemployment

We start with the record on growth. Figure 1 for the UK shows an average annual growth rate of 3 per cent from 1950 to 1973. The figures are low by international comparisons - Germany, Japan and France all did better - but high by historic ones. Since 1980, in contrast, the growth rate has fallen to an average of 2.2 per cent a year.[4]

This fall in the growth rate has been a global phenomenon. At 3.2 per cent, the

'Managed' v 'market capitalism': the record

Figure 1: The record on growth, UK
Average annual growth rate per period

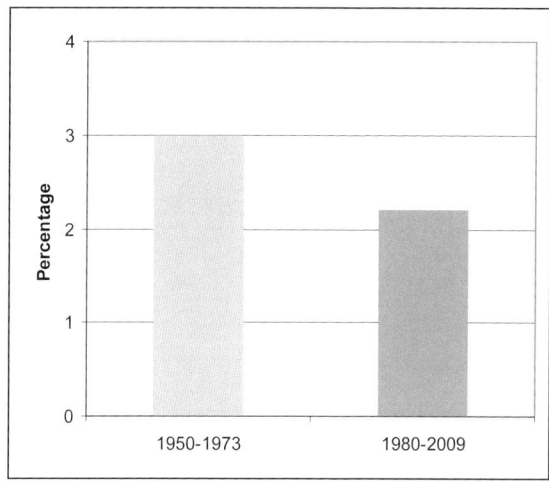

Source: Annual change in GDP, chained volume measure, seasonally adjusted (ONS series ABMI): http://www.statistics.gov.uk/statbase/TSDdownload2.asp

annual rate of real world growth was significantly lower from 1980 to 2009 than the 4.8 per cent from 1950 to 1973.[5] This pattern holds for all the major economies. The US, UK, Japan, Germany and France all experienced slower growth after 1980 than during the post-war era.[6]

Partly as a result of this slowing growth rate, the British economy, along with most high income economies, has been run at a much higher level of unemployment. In the two immediate post-war decades, the problem of the mass unemployment of the 1930s had been largely cracked. In the era of 'managed capitalism' from 1950 to 1973, as shown in figure 2, the UK unemployment rate averaged 1.6 per cent. This was perhaps the nearest the country has come to full employment, at least in the case of males.

Unemployment under 'market capitalism' has been much higher. It has averaged 7.8 per cent, nearly five times that of the earlier period. This is despite a steady fall in the share of national output accruing to wage-earners, from around 60 per cent at the end of the 1970s to 53 per cent by 2008.[7] Yet, according to the market theorists, a declining wage share would be an important source of job creation.

As unemployment has soared, it has also become increasingly concentrated, hitting some areas, regions and individuals much more heavily than others. As a result, the jobless are typically out of work for longer than in the past. In the UK the proportion

Figure 2: The record on unemployment
Unemployment Rate, 1950-2009, UK

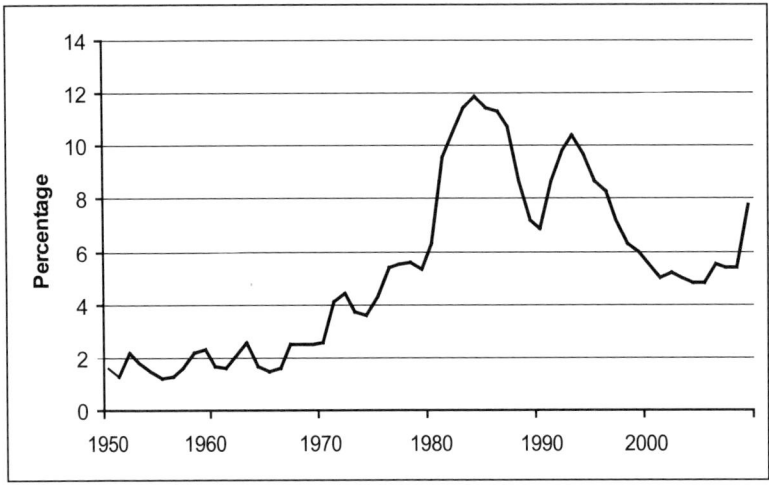

Source: The data from 1971-2009 is the ILO unemployment rate (series MGSX, second quarter), seasonally adjusted. The figures for 1950-1970 were provided by the ONS. Because of changes in definitions, the series before and after 1970 are not strictly comparable.

unemployed for more than a year in the period since 2000 has been nearly three times the level of the 1950s. At the end of 2010, it stood at close to 30 per cent.[8]

Of course, 'the golden age' of the post-war era with its high growth rates was aided by several factors in addition to the introduction of managed markets and Keynesian fine-tuning, notably the programmes of post-war re-construction and a rapid period of technical change. Nevertheless, controlled markets, capital controls, a stable international monetary system and steadily rising demand were important factors driving success. The period was, above all, evidence of how managed economies, with a mix of national and global controls over markets and the free flow of capital, can be highly successful.

The record on productivity

One of the most important measures of changing dynamism is what has happened to labour productivity - the growth of output per job. 'Productivity isn't everything', according to the American Nobel Economics Laureate, Paul Krugman, 'but in the

'Managed' v 'market capitalism': the record

long run it's almost everything'. And it is the poor record on productivity that lies behind the slowing growth rates of the last thirty years.

The architects of deregulation claimed that liberated product and labour markets would unleash a new spirit of enterprise, and close the UK's gap in productivity with the US and leading European nations. Yet the evidence is that freer markets, hands-off government and soaring corporate pay at the top have failed to engineer a significant improvement in Britain's productivity and innovation record.

In some ways Britain is more entrepreneurial. Business schools are booming and entrepreneurial aspirations have grown. Yet these aspirations have yet to be translated into a noticeable improvement in the quality of entrepreneurship. New business-start up rates have marginally improved and there has been a steady rise in the number of small businesses. But the rate of business failure has remained pretty static in recent years while the UK had fallen from seventh in the world competitiveness rankings (compiled by the World Economic Forum) in 1997 to thirteenth in 2009.[9]

Although productivity rates improved sharply in the 1980s in parts of manufacturing, this was largely because of the mass shedding of jobs at the time. Privatisation of state owned firms also led to improved productivity in several industries, such as steel, which lost close to half its workforce.[10] Overall, however, as shown in figure 3, productivity growth has deteriorated since 1980, averaging 1.9 per cent a year to 2008, compared with an annual average rise of 2.95 per cent from 1961 to 1973.

The slipping in the productivity rate during the 1970s and 1980s can perhaps be explained away by the economic difficulties of the 1970s and a delayed reaction to the impact of the dramatic switches in direction - deflation, privatisation and deregulation - of the 1980s. What is less easily explained by the new orthodoxy is why there was not an improved performance after 1990 from the freeing up of markets and lower inflation.

Despite leading the pack of rich nations when it came to de-regulation, the US also displayed a poor record from 1990. The country enjoyed a boost to productivity in the years of the late 1990s to the early 2000s - when it reached 2.5 per cent a year - a success which came to be viewed at the time as a justification for the opening up of markets. Nevertheless, the longer performance from 1990 cannot be described as

Figure 3: The record on productivity
Growth in productivity per annum, UK, percentages.

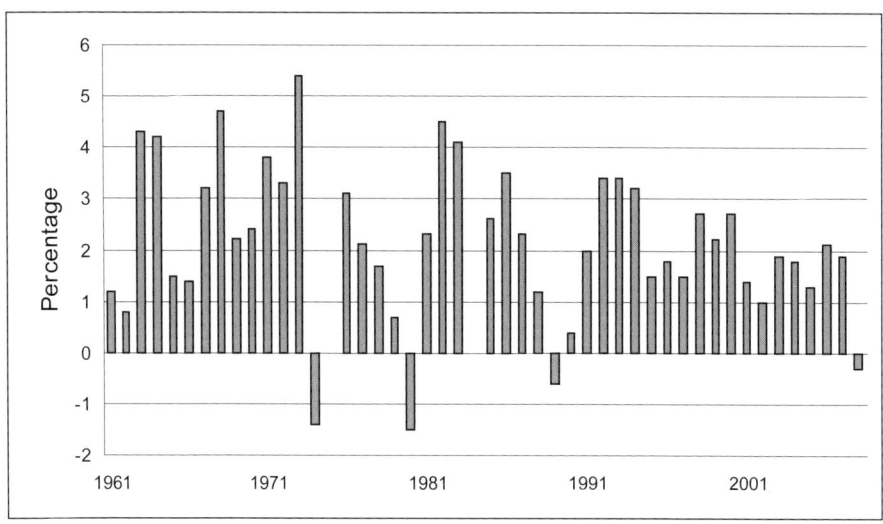

Source: ONS, output per job for whole economy (series LNNP). Comparable figures are not available pre-1961

outstanding. Productivity rose by an annual average of 1.9 per cent in the fourteen years to 2004, compared with just over 3 per cent from 1960 to 1973.[11]

Internationally, the UK has slightly closed the productivity gap with its main international competitors over the last two decades, but it still lags well behind the US, Germany and France. According to a study by the Economic and Social Research Council, the reasons include 'a relative failure to invest, failure to innovate, poor labour relations, trade distortions attributable to Empire, antagonism towards manufacturing, "short-termism" among business leaders and financial institutions, technological backwardness and lack of entrepreneurship'.[12]

Britain's weak record on productivity is in part due to the failure to translate the rising profit share that has occurred since the 1980s into productive investment.[13] Because of the low level of investment, Britain's infrastructure remains poor compared with its main competitors. Too many plants operate with antiquated systems, while levels of training have lagged behind other countries. Despite the introduction of freer markets, funding for training, research and development and

'Managed' v 'market capitalism': the record

innovation has slowed.[14] Manufacturing entrepreneurs like James Dyson who invest in engineers are the exception.

The evidence is of a strong link between R&D and related capital spending and added value, and eventually profitability.[15] Yet, apart from a handful of industries such as defence, pharmaceuticals and mobile phones, UK companies invest less in R&D, innovation and capital equipment than their international competitors. In most industries the levels of capital expenditure by foreign companies in Britain greatly exceed that of indigenous companies.[16] In the 1960s and 1970s, the UK's spending on R&D as a share of GDP was comparable to its leading competitors. Since then, the UK has slipped badly behind, and in 2005 spent a lower proportion than in 1973. In contrast, most leading economic nations increased their share of GDP spent on R&D. As one former leading industrialist has complained 'The British tragedy is that we have moved from a system of high R&D spend, accompanied by rotten management, to one of low R&D spend, accompanied by a different form of poor management!'.[17]

Boom and bust

A fourth test relates to economic volatility. One of the central tenets of the free market theorists was that markets would deliver greater stability. The Chicago-based Robert Lucas, one of the most influential of the new thinkers, with his 'rational expectations' theory of boom and bust, demonstrated that, with rational individuals, perfect capital markets and full information - assumptions at the heart of economic theory - governments would be irrelevant to the delivering of economic stability. In 2003, Lucas, who won the Nobel Prize for Economics in 1995, gave the Presidential Address at the annual meeting of the American Economic Association. 'The central problem of depression-prevention', he momentously explained to his audience, 'has been solved, for all practical purposes'.

By this he did not mean that the economic cycle had disappeared, or that the economy would not suffer occasional setbacks, just that the days of severe recession were over, and that economic fine-tuning was of no value. A year later, in February 2004, Ben Bernanke, a former Princeton Professor and soon to be appointed Chairman of the Federal Reserve, gave a speech called 'The Great Moderation', which made a similar point. Bernanke claimed that because of the apparent

Soundings

decline in the variability of both output and inflation from the late-1980s, modern macroeconomics had moderated the problem of the business cycle. According to these accounts, from two of the leading economic theorists in the US, the disaster of 2008-2009 should not have happened.

Despite the theorists' critique of the role of state intervention, active intervention to moderate the business cycle had a strong track record in the post-war era. As the American economist Hyman Minsky observed in 1982, 'The most significant economic event of the era since World War II is something that has not happened: there has not been a deep and long-lasting depression'.[18] Despite claims that the injection of market forces would reduce the capitalist tendency towards instability, the world became a more turbulent place in the next three decades than in the immediate post-war period.

The IMF has generally been reluctant to use the word recession, but when forced, its chief economists have defined a 'global recession' informally as a year with a global growth average of less than 3 per cent. This is because while 3 per cent would be a strong rate for rich countries, emerging market economies have much higher 'normal' growth rates. In these countries a fall in growth to below a figure of 3 to 4 per cent is similar in impact to negative growth in rich economies.

On this definition, the world has experienced no less than five recessions since 1980. Moreover, the busts have been getting steadily larger. In contrast, as shown by Robert Skidelsky, political economist and biographer of Keynes, there were no global recessions in the era of managed capitalism - the world did not record a single year from 1950-1973 when growth fell below 3 per cent.[19]

On the alternative, more conventional definition of a recession - negative real growth in two successive quarters - this pattern still holds. There have been more and deeper recessions since 1980 than between 1950 and 1973.[20] Take the UK economy. Although it experienced a number of exchange rate and stop-go crises in the two decades from 1950, there were only three shallow and short-lived recessions in this period. As shown in figure 4, there was one in 1956, when output fell by 1.4 per cent over three quarters; one in 1957, when output fell by 0.9 per cent over two quarters; and then one in 1961, when it fell by 0.7 per cent over two quarters.[21]

In contrast, the period since 1980 has been distinguished by more frequent, more prolonged and more severe economic shocks than the earlier period, with

'Managed' v 'market capitalism': the record

Figure 4: The record on recessions
Post-war recessions in the UK, percentage fall in output

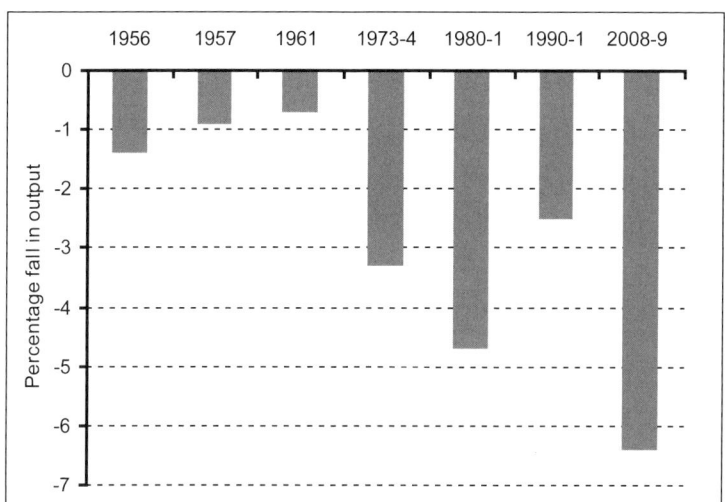

Source: Office for National Statistics, GDP at market prices, chained volume index, percentage change, quarter on previous quarter, YBEZ. See also Office for NationalStatistics, 'Output and Expenditure in the Last Three UK Recessions', *Economic and Labour Market Review*, August 2010.

three deep-seated recessions. Specifically, in 1980-1981 when output fell by 4.7 per cent (over five quarters); 1990-1991, when it fell by 2.5 per cent (over five quarters); and 2008-2009 when it fell by 6.4 per cent (over six quarters).

Not only have the UK and the world experienced more and deeper recessions; the crises of recent times have had very different origins. Earlier post-war dips (mild as they were by comparison) were triggered by deflationary policies that were needed to get inflation under control (as was that of 1980-1982). The most recent recessions have had nothing to do with inflation (or soaring wage demands). They have had much more to do with rising asset prices, driven by excess profits and unsustainable credit, and fuelled by financial deregulation.[22]

This has also been the main cause of the upsurge in financial crises, most of them associated with a torrent of currency, stock or property speculation. In the two decades from 1950 there were no banking crises and relatively few financial crises. Since the end of the 1970s, the number of such crises has mushroomed. As *Financial Times* columnist Martin Wolf has put it, 'financial liberalisation and financial crises

Soundings

go together like a horse and carriage'.[23]

From the beginning of the 1980s, the number of banking failures in the US started rising sharply, a problem exacerbated by the impact of bank deregulation.[24] In October 1987, the world's leading stock markets crashed, their largest fall in a day since the crash of 1929. A serious fall-out for the world economy was only averted by a huge injection of global liquidity. In 1989, the bursting of a serious property bubble in Japan, triggered by a series of bank liquidity crises, led to a decade-long period of deflation and a sustained collapse in Japanese shares prices. It had been preceded by a decade of rising profits (which had risen to 40 per cent of output) and soaring assert prices.[25] Between 1990 and 1992, Norway, Sweden and Finland all suffered a banking crisis sparked by a similar property boom, deregulation of financial services, and excessive lending by banks. Again, only decisive action by the national governments prevented a more prolonged fall-out.

Five years later, the Asian currency crisis, driven by financial over-reach, caused mayhem across south-east Asia when currency speculators pulled billions out of Asian currency markets. In 2000, the collapse of the dot.com bubble brought world stock markets crashing once again.

As the age of stability gave way to the age of turbulence, the chronic economic crisis that hit the global economy in 2008 provided the ultimate test of the effectiveness of the near thirty-year long experiment in market capitalism. It was a test that resulted in dramatic failure. Yet, according to the market theorists, the economic meltdown of 2008-2009 should not have happened. The promise of self-regulating markets might have worked in the computerised mathematical models of the neoliberal economic theorists, but they failed in the real world.

Even on the basis of its own goals, the economic strategy of the last thirty years can claim only one success, the taming of inflation. On all other goals, it has failed. Instead, the most marked legacy of the market experiment has been a persistent rise in inequality, one so sharp that it has sent the wealth and income gap in the United Kingdom and the United States back to levels last seen in the inter-war years. Far from being a mechanism for delivering economic success, the primary function of the Anglo-Saxon economic model, it seems, has been to hand power to a new generation of business executives and financiers who have used it to enrich themselves, irrespective of the consequences for the economy and the workforce.

'Managed' v 'market capitalism': the record

This is a view no longer confined to critics of the market. In an article in the *Daily Telegraph* (22.7.11), entitled 'I'm Starting to think the Left Might be Right After All', Charles Moore, the former editor of the paper, examined whether 'what the Right calls "the free market" is actually a set-up'. His conclusion:

> It turns out ... that a system purporting to advance the many has been perverted in order to enrich the few. The global banking system is an adventure playground for the participants, complete with spongy, health-and-safety approved flooring so that they bounce when they fall off. The role of the rest of us is simply to pay.

Yet, despite its record, and the growing list of sceptics, the market orthodoxy remains largely intact. The overwhelming virtues of markets are still being taught in business schools and economic departments. State industrial policy that could provide the means to hasten economic recovery is shunned. The Treasury remains little more than an outpost of the City, while the Coalition government believes that the solution to Britain's fragile economy lies in another boost of market freedom, with further restrictions on workplace rights. The lesson of the last thirty years, spelt out so clearly by Charles Moore, that what the British economy needs is a greatly reformed model of capitalism, seems yet to have been learned.

Stewart Lansley is a research fellow at the Townsend Centre for International Poverty Research, University of Bristol, and the author of *The Cost of Inequality: Three Decades of the Super-Rich and the Economy*, Gibson Square 2011.

Notes

1. IMF, *World Economic Outlook, Database*, April 2009.

2. T. Morgan, 'No Way Out', *Tullett Prebon Strategy Note 23*, 2011.

3. Although this comparison misses 1974-1979, this period was a special case which saw the first serious recession of the post-war era, one ushered in by the OPEC shock. Moreover, the application of market principles did not start until Margaret Thatcher and Ronald Reagan were in power. However, if the period

of 'managed capitalism' was extended to take in the period 1974 to 1979, the comparisons would not be significantly different.

4. Annual change in GDP, chained volume measure, seasonally adjusted (Office for National Statistics, series ABMI): www.statistics.gov.uk/statbase/TSDdownload2.asp.

5. GDP adjusted for inflation.

6. R. Skidelsky, *Keynes: The Return of the Master*, Allen Lane 2009, pp118-120.

7. See S. Lansley, *The Cost of Inequality: Three Decades of the Super-Rich and the Economy*, Gibson Square 2011, chapter 2.

8. For the 1950s to the 1980s, *Social Justice*, Report of the Social Justice Commission, Vintage 1994; for the 1990s and 2000s, ONS: www.statistics.gov.uk/elmr/03_10/downloads/Table2_09.xls.

9. World Economic Forum, *The Global Competitiveness Report, 2009-10*, 2009.

10. G.L. Bernstein, *The Myth of Decline*, Pimlico, 2004, p572.

11. *The Myth of Decline*; and A. Glyn, *Capitalism Unleashed*, OUP 2006, p131.

12. ESRC, *The UK's Productivity Gap*, ESRC Seminar Series, 2004; see also Office for Fair Trading, *Productivity and Competition*, 2007.

13. *The Cost of Inequality*, chapter 2.

14. N. Bloom & R. Griffiths, 'The Internationalisation of UK R&D', *Fiscal Studies*, 2001, Vol 22, No 3.

15. 'Internationalisation of UK R&D'.

16. *The Myth of Decline*, pp537, 575.

17. Don Young, having their cake.com.

18. Quoted in Niall Ferguson, *The Ascent of Money*, Allen Lane 2008, p164.

19. *Keynes: The Return of the Master*, p119.

20. This would be true even if the period was extended to take in the 1974-5 global recession.

21. GDP at market prices, chained volume index, percentage change per quarter (YBEZ).

'Managed' v 'market capitalism': the record

22. *The Cost of Inequality*, chapter 11.

23. M. Wolf, 'This time will never be different', *Financial Times*, 28.8.09.

24. D. Moss, 'An Ounce of Prevention', *Harvard Magazine*, October 2009.

25. Gerald Holtham, 'Workers of the World Compete', *Prospect*, December 2008.

Soundings
is now freely available online to all subscribers

Benefits include:

- ♦ Document to document linking using live references, for fast, reliable access to wider, related literature.
- ♦ Journal content that is fully searchable, across full text, abstracts, titles, TOCs and figures.
- ♦ Live links to and from major Abstract and Indexing resources to aid research.
- ♦ The ability to conduct full-text searching across multiple journals, giving you a wider view of the research that counts.
- ♦ Powerful TOC alerting services that keep you up to date with the latest research.

**Set up access now at:
www.ingentaselect.com/register.htm**

and follow the online instructions*

Subscription Enquiries:
help@ingenta.com

*Access is provided by Ingenta Select, an Ingenta website

Soundings